Heirloom Miniatures

By Tina M. Gravatt

American Quilter's Society
P.O. Box 3290
Paducah, KY 42002-3290

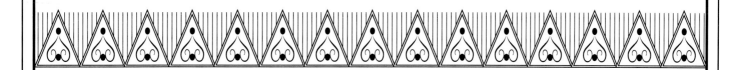

This book is dedicated to
Carrie Anne Gravatt,
without whom there wouldn't be even one
miniature quilt in my home!

TABLE OF CONTENTS

FOREWORD

Spending months making a quilt that is only 19" x 24" is a task I relish. More than that, I devote most of my waking hours and sometimes even time in my sleep to it. But hand me a sheet of white paper and ask me to put down my thoughts and ideas on it, and I recoil like a threatened animal. I want to thank my family for understanding both of these facts and supporting me in all my endeavors. They even put up with me when I short circuit and threaten to throw the typewriter across the room.

My family is not a traditional one. I share a three-story Brownstone with my younger daughter, Carrie Anne and a fellow artist and friend, Sheila A. Rosenfield. We share space, cooking and cleaning chores, family outings, support and the agonies of any household.

Shelia has Multiple Sclerosis but through it all continues to do very creative silk screen prints and most of my mathematical calculations. I came to her and said, "I want to do a Mariner's compass quilt in miniature." She said, "What's a Mariner's compass?" From that beginning she has learned almost as many quilt patterns as I have. She can reduce a pattern, pieced or appliqued, from any size down to the 3" or less that I need, and then makes the templates and quilting patterns. Without her help and support, the miniature quilts would never have been as accurate and precise as they are.

Carrie, who is now 16, is the reason behind the miniature quilts in this book. If she hadn't been a cute "con artist" I should never have made a miniature quilt. Beyond that fact, however, is more. She is a loving and kind person who is always there for a hug when I'm feeling low. She is clever and can spot a mistake in a quilt from across the room, not that I'm glad to know there is one. She is a skilled writer and has helped proofread all my manuscripts, corrected my phraseology, and done the same for my spelling.

I'd also like to acknowledge the support and encouragement of my parents. Mom and Dad are always there when I need them. No matter what I ask, they find a way to help. They may not have known what a quilt was 16 years ago when I started quiltmaking, but they very quickly learned and share my interests and joys. I love them and thank them for everything they have been to me over the years.

To my quilting group, the "Wild Geese Quilters" of Philadelphia, Pennsylvania, thanks for all your support of my work. They are always the first to see the newest miniature quilt and praise it, and the first to encourage me to start the next one. A special thank you to Wild Goose, Florence Davis, who assisted with my manuscript editing.

There is one other group of quilters that I would also like to thank. They are the women who have for hundreds of years taken a functional art, born of necessity, and made it into an art form that is now exhibited in art museums and historical societies. Sometimes these old quilts were made as masterpieces for future generations to enjoy; but most often the quilts were functional ones with love stitched into every piece. It is from these quilts that I have taken my inspiration and it is to these quilters that I am indebted, for without them I would never have found my life's work and love.

Last but not least, a special thank you to Meredith Schroeder and the American Quilter's Society for putting into print what we quilters stitch into each quilt.

INTRODUCTION

You may wonder how I got started making heirloom miniature quilts. Like many events, I stumbled into making them by accident.

My daughter, Carrie Anne, then age 12, hinted for a doll bed as a Christmas present. As an indulgent parent, I decided to order a doll bed kit from a magazine. Then I set about designing and completing a miniature crazy quilt for it. When the bed arrived, I assembled it and made mattresses, pillows, linens and a blanket. The total effect of quilt, bed, etc. was quite striking and very successful.

I began to think about other traditional patchwork patterns which might be fun to make in miniature. I decided to use the hexagon shape for a Grandmother's Flower Garden variation, a design I had always admired but had not wished to spend the rest of my life constructing. Working in ½" on a side hexagons was quite a challenge, but the resulting miniature was even more successful than the first.

Since the quilt represented five weeks of work and contained 512 hexagons, all sewn by hand, it had become more than a child's plaything. Not only did I keep it, but I went to the local toy store and bought myself a doll bed! The potential for miniatures was beginning to dawn on me.

I had always been a student of the history of quilts, and I began combining the historical research with the making of the small quilts. Constructing historically accurate miniature quilts allows the quiltmaker to experiment. Color and fabrics can be studied to find ones that look old and faded much the same as the old quilt, or strong colors can be chosen to capture the feeling of the quilt as it might have appeared when it had been first made. The graphic impact of the late 19th century can be copied in a miniature quilt with dynamic results. Sometimes the quiltmaker may choose a miniature quilt which will involve hand embroidery, even stuffed work or trapunto. Almost any quilt that can be made in the full-bed size can be reinterpreted in miniature providing the quiltmaker with the opportunity to try out many different patterns and techniques. For some of us quilters, these small quilts provide the opportunity to make all the many types of quilts that one could ever want to make and be able to do so within one's lifetime.

The miniature quilts that I have selected for this book are like traveling through time. The first quilt is a basic, beginner's pattern which dates back in American quilting history to at least the 18th century. I have included some history on each quilt and the reader will learn the approximate dates of popularity for each. Seventeen quilts later will bring the reader into the 20th century with the Art Deco style of Grandmother's Fans. General directions are included to help the quiltmaker use various techniques in producing these quilts with specific instructions, patterns and templates included.

Here's hoping that some quilters who may not have thought miniatures were for them will now be tempted to give them a try.

Part I

The Quilts & Their Histories

NINE PATCH (Plate I)
Time Period: Early-Present

Since patchwork was primarily a woman's task, and women's history was not as factually or fully recorded as that of men, we may never know which was the first patchwork pattern. Certainly a basic four or nine patch would seem to be the answer. They were patterns that were easy to piece without bias seams or difficult assembly.

Little girls and even boys began sewing at an early age, three or four years. To teach them their needlework skills, and to help perfect them, a basic pattern would have been their first patchwork. Children could be given the small scraps, useless for larger projects, to be used in their piecing. There are many surviving old quilt blocks in the four and nine patch patterns which exhibit the crude and rudimentary skills of beginning needleworkers.

I've chosen to make my miniature nine patch appear as if it might have been made in the early 1840's. American-printed calicoes were then becoming abundant and many quilters, of all economic classes, could afford them. The prints I've used are composed of stylized flowers, squiggles, stripes, and dots. The color scheme is in greens, brown, and reds.

I like small quilts to have the same sort of visual interest as a large quilt. I selected a nine patch pattern in which all of the pieces were not the same size. I added to this effect by having two different (though similarly colored) blocks set on the diagonal, to make the quilt more graphic and dynamic. By introducing a fifth color in the outside triangles, a border effect was achieved which helps to draw the viewer's eye into the piece. A double border was attached to look like the borders in the old quilts and a binding of the triangles' color fools the eye into thinking that a third border has been added.

All of these seemingly contemporary design tricks can be seen in the old 19th century quilts. Sometimes the quiltmaker created differently colored triangles, blocks or borders because of a shortage of fabric. Whatever the reason, the results were enviable and should be incorporated in the quilts of today, big or small.

GEESE IN FLIGHT (Plate II)
Time Period : 1820-Present

Geese in Flight is also an old pattern, another beginner's quilt. It is for the quiltmaker who has mastered the skills and accuracy of a four or nine patch and is now ready to tackle the bias edge(s) of a triangle, the only pattern shape used in this quilt.

Since relatively small shapes are used in the two outside triangles, this pattern is most often seen as a scrap quilt. Even in the early quilts of the first quarter of the 19th century scraps were used, but the "left-overs" contained in those quilts were often lovely imported chintzes.

In miniature, one can put together different and interesting fabrics as in the old quilts; however, the size of each piece is quite small, often only an inch or so. Because of this, it is not possible for the quilt viewer to linger over each and every fabric, focusing on its individual merits. In order to keep the quilt from becoming boring, a creative approach to the stripping between the rows is important. To accomplish this, I used an idea from a circa 1825 Geese in Flight quilt which used varying width stripes. The quiltmaker had used a dynamic red striped chintz to separate her geese and the effect was most striking.

When adding borders to miniature quilts, the temptation is to put them on and butt joint the corners, as in many old quilts. However, in a quilt this small, the effect looks more like carelessness or inadequate planning. I have found that mitering the corners of the borders gives a more sophisticated and thoughtful finish to the quilt. When using border prints, mitering the corners also provides a 90° turning that can be interesting and create secondary focal points for the quilt. Always be sure, however, not to let them dominate the patchwork or applique of the quilt itself.

FOUR EAGLES (Plate III)
Time Period: 1840-1900

The American eagle has appeared on a large number of quilts throughout the 19th century. The first ones appeared shortly after the eagle was made our national emblem by the new Congress. By the 1840's an arrangement of four eagles around a center motif became so popular with quiltmakers that it was duplicated for decades, causing some quilt historians to suspect that kit quilts existed far earlier than imagined.

With the format remaining the same in all these quilts, the quiltmakers sought to make the design their own by modifying the center motifs and altering the border arrangements. Sometimes the quilts had multiple borders, other times they were pieced or appliqued. But the easiest way to personalize such a quilt was to change the items held in the eagles' beaks and claws. There are quilts where eagles are holding arrows, firecrackers, flowers, olive branches, and there is one antique quilt from Pennsylvania, circa 1885-1895, where the eagles seem to be smoking cigars! [1]

My quilt represents the traditional placement of the eagles and has double cog-like wheels in the center. Each eagle holds an olive branch in its beak and they have been quilted to make the eagles' chests appear shield-like. The colors are the traditional mid-19th century ones of red, white, yellow, and green. The pieced sawtooth border repeats the green fabric from the center and provides punch and vitality to this classic quilt. I was most fortunate to find a red stripe that was in scale with the miniature size of my eagles. It provides them with the patriotic folk-art look of the old quilts.

No large quilt is complete until it has been quilted, and neither is a miniature. The primary quilting on this piece is in diagonal rows, ½" apart. There is also quilting around all the applique shapes and in a double and single circular pattern within the cogs in the center.

FRIENDSHIP (Plate IV)
Time Period: 1840-1860

Friendship quilts were popular during many time periods of American quilting history, but their zenith was during the 1840's and 50's. In these quilts, many different patchwork patterns were used, the only consistent feature being a space for signature or sentiment. The fad was popular everywhere, from New England to the Midwest and in the southern states where elegant album-style quilts were made.

A small part of the friendship quilt's popularity can be attributed to the newly developed inks which were both permanent and safe for use on textiles. Women had little to call their own; land deeds, real estate, and important legal documents were all in their husband's name. Prior to 1850 only "heads of families" were listed

on census records. Women needed something of their own, private yet functional, a record of their time on earth and of their friends and families. Album books were very popular, but it was so much more personal to have a piece of "Aunt Bertha's wedding dress" or the babies' first pants, which these quilts provided.

America was on the move, ever westward, and many women left their mothers, aunts, uncles, and cousins to travel with their husbands, hundreds and even thousands of miles from home. How comforting it would have been to have a quilt on your bed with family and friend's names, and perhaps even their best wishes for the trip through life. "Remember me" was a very significant phrase to a pioneer woman.

My friendship quilt uses the album patch block and the colors chosen, pinks, grays, blues, reds, greens, browns, and salmon, are taken from a quilt made by the Crosby family of Milford, NH, circa 1849.[2] The original quilt was designed for a four poster bed and is cut out at the bottom to allow the quilt to drape smoothly within the posts. A bold sashing of salmon was used in both the original and mine and the same fabric was brought out into the border triangles at the top of the quilt.

On mine the squares are signed using a permanent pen, with names and when possible birth dates of my children, parents, grandparents, and great-grandparents, uncles, and cousins. By leaving blank squares, I will be able to add grandchildren and great-grandchildren.

ROSE OF SHARON (Plate V)
Time Period: 1850-1870

Quiltmakers drew upon many sources for the names of their quilt patterns; animal names, place names, politicians, patriotic slogans, and the Bible were some of the common themes. This last category was perhaps the most popular.

In "The Song of Solomon" the Shulamite princess speaks of herself as "the rose of Sharon." From these lines, quiltmakers drew inspiration for perhaps their finest quilt, the engagement or wedding quilt.

These quilts, whether made by the bride herself or by her family, would often contain the best workmanship the quiltmaker could exhibit. The quilts would be shown to many people and be treasured for an entire lifetime, so anything but one's best work would be inappropriate. Many times hearts and love birds were included, if not in the design of the quilt itself, then in the quilting.

The Rose of Sharon pattern was made over such a

long period of time that there is not one pattern but hundreds, with each quiltmaker putting herself, her experiences and skills into the rose design.

My interpretation is styled after the Southern applique masterpieces of the mid-19th century. It contains a rose motif, stuffed in the center flower and petal areas. The small buds, leaves and vines are left unstuffed although they appear to be treated in the same way. This effect was achieved by using stipple quilting, a technique which involves filling the entire background areas with quilting stitches ⅛" apart. Because there is so much quilting, the background areas become flat and the areas left unquilted "puff up" and appear stuffed. As in the old Rose of Sharon quilts, I wanted to use my most expert needlework skills and create a masterpiece quilt.

OAK LEAVES (Plate VI)
Time Period: 1840-1860

Most all the giant oak trees of America are long gone, but the quiltmakers of the mid-19th century immortalized them with many different patterns. I chose a simple one whose design shape came from a circa 1860 quilt that I own.

My old quilt is composed of 16" square blocks of eight different green fabrics. Some of them are in the old Queen Victoria green (a yellow/green) not seen today. The sashings on the quilt are 2½" wide and there are four blocks across and the same number down. One edge has an applied twill binding not found on the other three sides and may indicate that it was "cut down" to its existing dimensions. The fabric used in the sashing appears to be a red and white print, but upon closer examination, the white dots are actually holes caused by the chemicals of the old dyes eating through the fabric.

Copying an old quilt in miniature required much decision making. I chose to use green fabrics that are currently available on the market and used four different prints and colors to simulate the variations that exist in my old quilt. I also decided to give my quilt the same number of blocks in the same arrangement as the old one. I even kept the sashing's polka dot effect by using a red with white dot print.

HEXAGONS (Plate VII & VIII)
Time Period: 1870-1880

The crusaders brought the hexagon shape from the Middle East to Europe where it has long since been associated with English patchwork. In America hexagons were prevalent during the late Victorian era and in the early years of the 20th century.

A patch with six sides was more difficult to piece than one with only four. The easiest method for handling hexagons was to cut papers to the finished size and wrap the fabric over it, basting in place. This method was long and tedious and not as appealing as the more standard patchwork construction technique. Nonetheless, beautiful hexagon quilts from the 1870's and 80's survive today. There were many different arrangements, the most popular being Grandmother's Flower Garden.

In my hexagon quilts, I've created both a garden-like look and a star pattern. Each quilt was thoroughly planned on paper before a piece of fabric was cut. Even though the shapes are small, ½" and ⁵⁄₁₆" on a side, they are not difficult to construct as piecing with paper ensures excellent accuracy and fine results. They are very portable and can be taken along to meetings, doctors' offices, etc. It is very satisfying to be able to accomplish the piecing of many hexagons while waiting for some event to occur.

CRAZY (Plate IX)
Time Period: 1870-1900

Perhaps the greatest fad of the Victorian era was the crazy "quilt." (Since most of these quilts did not contain any batting or filler and were not quilted, they are not true quilts.) These parlor or bed decorations commanded much time, energy and needlework skill.

The lady's magazines of the day were filled with instructions and ideas for the making and decorating of these popular quilts. No proper homemaker of the day would be without one. The old cliche, "the more, the merrier" best describes the quiltmaker's approach to these quilts. All sorts of designs, slogans, and pictures can be found on the old ones, along with lace, ribbons, trims and even beading.

I used sateen, taffeta, moire and velvet for my fabrics and embellished them with old embroidery patterns taken from crazy quilts of the period. All the spaces have been filled in and all seam lines covered with embroidery stitches. The quilt has a few tacking stitches to keep the backing from separating from the front, but it is not tied or quilted.

YO-YO (Plate X)
Time Period: 1880-1930

Along with the quilt craze came the yo-yo style of parlor throw or pillow covering. While the crazy quilt fad died out between 1900 and 1920, yo-yos continued their popularity well into the 1940's.

To make these, fabric was cut into round circles and then a basting stitch was used to draw the circle up into the yo-yo shape. Sometimes the "quilts" were lined, other times, not. Often they were made from scraps and every color in the rainbow might be present in just one quilt.

I chose three different lavender prints which I highlighted with a beige print and a black and lavender fabric. The result is soft and very feminine. Because each yo-yo is the size of a dime, from a distance the quilt looks more like crochet work than yo-yos. I even know someone who thinks they look like 238 mice shower caps!

LOG CABIN VARIATION (Plate XI)
Time Period: 1880-1890

The idea for this miniature came from a circa 1880's wool challis quilt. The design has the appearance of being one large log cabin block with six extra "logs" at the top. Perhaps the reason for these strips were to make the quilt long enough to fit a particular bed and/or add interest over the pillow area.

Although the design is a simple one and the construction quite easy, this quilt can become more interesting by the use of either old or reproduction fabrics. For several years, cloth manufacturers have been reprinting some of the fabric designs of the late 19th century. I used seven different reprints in my quilt and 11 old fabrics dating from 1880 through 1920. The blending of the two fabric types, old and new, are most effective and give the quilt a soft, semi-used, late 19th century look much like the original.

ONE PATCH SCRAP (Plate XII)
Time Period: 1880-1900

Survival on a pioneering homestead meant resourcefulness and frugality. Scrap quilts are surviving remnants of the old cliche "waste not, want not." This miniature is based on a quilt made by Clara Countryman of Wyoming, Ohio in the 1880's.[3] The original quilt must have required a lifetime of scraps from many clothing and household projects.

My quilt represents about 15 years of my personal remnants from numerous quilting and sewing projects. It contains 421 one-inch pieces set on the diagonal. It is great fun to look at this quilt and see many old "friends" from my past.

Another benefit of a quilt of this sort is that it provides the maker with the opportunity to make a "small" dent in her or his personal scrap bag.

ROSE DREAM (Plate XIII)
Time Period: 1900-1920

This quilt has at least two names. One is True Lover's Knot, the other, Rose Dream, which I have chosen to call my quilt. My miniature is an exact copy of a quilt by that name made by Frances Umbach Hoffman of Dodge City, Kansas in 1920.[1]

The dramatic effect of two-color quilts has long been known, blue and white and red and white being the most popular combinations. The late 19th century

saw many of these quilts with the red and white color scheme predominating. I chose a red print with black squiggly lines rather than a solid fabric because the quilt obtains a third dimension from the print even before the quilting stitches are added.

As with the hexagon style of patchwork, this design requires extreme accuracy to look its best. I chose the paper piecing technique for its construction, but this method leaves all the seams pressed open, so I designed my quilting to be ¼" away from all seams and to echo the shapes of the patches, except for the four patches where diagonal lines were used.

GRANDMOTHER'S FAN (Plate XIV)
Time Period: 1920-1940

Fan patterns first appeared in the mid-19th century with the opening of the trade routes to the Orient. Their popularity was further enhanced by the new awareness of oriental design brought about by the objects displayed in the Japanese Pavilion at the Philadelphia Centennial in 1876. Many fans, embroidered or pieced, appear on the crazy quilts of the 1880's. By the 1920's and 30's fans had regained their former glory, and the old fan patterns, with a modern Art Deco look, were now being called Grandmother's Fans.

The printed fabrics used in my quilt are all genuine 1930's fabrics. Frequently, 1930's quilts were made in the pastel colors of lavender, Nile green, and the pink which I used in the border. Wide, picture frame-like border treatments using complex quilting patterns, like the double cable, were very popular. The diagonal setting of the blocks is what gives this quilt its strong Art Deco look.

CHINESE COINS (Plate XV)
Time Period: 1880-1940

The name for this quilt is said to be the Amish interpretation of the Chinese adding machine or abacus. The beauty of this style of quilt comes not from the pattern pieces, the shapes being simply bars of varying widths sewed together without thought to accuracy or uniformity; but rather in the color selections and pairings. It is fun to experiment with many different solid colors and shades and to combine them in pairs until a pleasing arrangement is achieved.

Since precision piecing is not necessary, this quilt pattern is an excellent one to make with children.

PRINCESS FEATHER (Plate XVI)
Time Period: 1870-1910

This applique design was a popular Pennsylvania German pattern which was made either as multi-block repeats or as one large overall motif. The colors were usually yellow, green and red, but in the last decade of the 19th century some of these quilts were made in yellow, pink, and blue.

The inspiration for this pattern has been attributed to several sources. One theory is that it comes from the old English feather quilting patterns inspired by the puffy plumed feathers of the early 17th century Cavaliers' hats. The other suggestion is that the Princess Feather pattern is an adaptation of the three plumes on the Prince of Wales' coat of arms. No matter what the source, it was a quilt that was a Pennsylvania tradition for many years.

I chose muted colors for my miniature so that it would look old and a bit faded. The border is an old pieced design called zigzag and carries the motion of the feather motif from the center of the quilt to the outside, containing the movement without stopping it.

HAWAIIAN-KAMIKANI KAILI ALOHA (Plate XVII)
Time Period: 1850-Present

Quilting was introduced into the Hawaiian Islands on April 3, 1820 by missionaries from New England. That first sewing and quilting session is recorded in the ship's log and gives us an idea how important quilts were in the culture of the day.

The Hawaiian natives developed this new art form into means of communicating the natural beauty of their native land. Traditional patterns abound for all types of flowers and foliage plants. This pattern, Kamikani Kaili Aloha, is said to represent the lush tropical foliage being blown by the soft trade winds. I modified the original pattern so that it now fits a 15" space. To create the border, I did as the Hawaiians do, took two shapes from the center design and paper-folded them into a repeat so that only one piece of fabric was used as the border pattern.

Frequently the old Hawaiian quilts are only two colors. I chose green for my "foliage" and white for the background. For this style quilt, it is important to have a good contrast between the two colors chosen. The quilting is in rows ¼" apart, echoing the shapes of the applique and its background. It was quite common to use echo quilting on the Hawaiian quilts of the late 19th century.

Heirloom Miniatures

COLOR PLATE SECTION

Plate I. **NINE PATCH**, 15½" x 18½", ©1987.

Plate II. **GEESE IN FLIGHT**, 19" x 24", ©1986.

Plate III. **FOUR EAGLES,** 20" x 20", ©1986.

Plate IV. **FRIENDSHIP**, 25½" x 31", ©1988.

Plate V. **ROSE OF SHARON**, 20" x 20", ©1986.

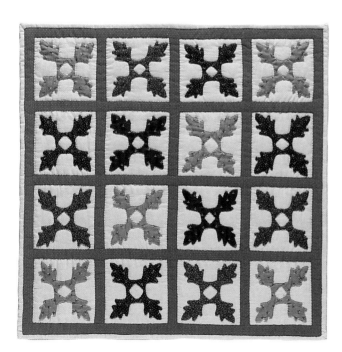

Plate VI. **OAK LEAVES,** 17" x 17", ©1987.

Plate VII. **SUMMER GARDEN**, 19½ x 20½", ©1985.

Plate VIII. **SHIMMERING STAR**, 8" x 7½",©1987.

Plate IX. **CRAZY,** 18" x 13½", ©1986.

Plate X. **YO-YO,** 9½" x 11½", ©1986.

Plate XI. **LOG CABIN VARIATION**, 16" x 20", ©1988.

Plate XII. **ONE PATCH SCRAP**, 20" x 20", ©1987.

Plate XIII. **ROSE DREAM,** 22" x 25", ©1988.

Plate XIV. **GRANDMOTHER'S FANS**, 18" x 22", ©1986.

Plate XV. **CHINESE COINS**, 17" x 23", ©1986.

Plate XVI. **PRINCESS FEATHER**, 20" x 20", ©1987.

Plate XVII. **KAMIKANI KAILI ALOHA,** 20" x 20", ©1986.

Part II

Making the Quilts

GENERAL INSTRUCTIONS

The instructions given here are not meant to be complete, "how to make a quilt from scratch" information. There are many books written on that subject already in the marketplace. The directions included here are for the purpose of instructing the quiltmaker in creating historically accurate miniature quilts. Of course, some of the information is also relevant to large scale projects as well, but the primary focus of these directions is to help the quiltmaker through the various problems that occur when working in miniature. Titles and authors of books with specific information, such as hand quilting, embroidery, etc. are included in the bibliography for your assistance.

PLANNING

Designing a miniature quilt requires the same considerations and decisions as those of a full-size quilt. If the miniature is being designed for use on a specific doll bed, however, some additional problems arise.

Doll beds, old and new, come in many sizes and shapes, and require the quilt to fit them perfectly, if it is to be successful. In other words, a well-done heirloom miniature is one which in a photograph would be indistinguishable from a large quilt. The miniature should drape and fold softly like a large quilt, should have a focal point and interest over the pillow area, and include borders which enhance and do not simply "end-off" the quilt.

To make the quiltmaker's job easier, I have developed a technique to produce on paper the proportions of the finished quilt. First, the quiltmaker must construct all the bedding that will go on the doll bed; i.e. mattress(es), pillow(s), sheet(s), blanket, etc. After these have been placed on the bed, measurements can be made of the various spaces that will be contained in the finished quilt.

Measure:

A. length of bed from headboard to footboard
B. width of bed from side to side of mattress
C. "tuck in" at the head of the bed, depth and width
D. "tuck in" at the foot of the bed, depth and width
E. distance from top of mattress to "floor" or however long you want the sides to be.

See Figs. 1 and 2.

Draw each of these sets of measurements on drawing or construction paper and cut them out. Tape each section to the center section so that the result is Fig. 3.

All the dimensions of the design areas of the quilt are now visible and it is easy to plan the specific size

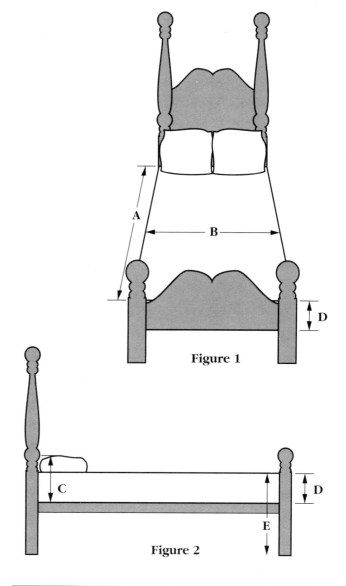

Figure 1

Figure 2

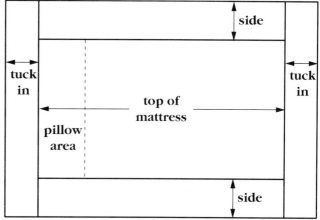

Figure 3

blocks necessary to fill these spaces. No need to fret over whether a 3" block for the border will work; the quiltmaker only needs to look at the side areas on her plan to know the answer. This technique is not limited to those who want to make their miniature quilt for a doll bed; it works just as well for someone planning a miniature quilt for the wall. The only difference is that the quiltmaker is the one who decides on the size of the various proportions within the quilt.

A small quilt, like a large one, should be exciting and dynamic as well as balanced and in proportion if it is to be successful. By using the paper diagram technique, it is easy to plan a patchwork or applique pattern to fit any size doll bed or wall hanging. Of course, compromises may have to be made between the ideal pattern and realities of actual space; this method, however, makes those decisions easier.

FABRIC

Weight and Weave:

Loose weaves and gauze-like fabrics are usually unsuitable for miniature work. When handling pieces of fabric 1" squares or smaller, fraying can become a problem and the additional difficulty of handling a loose weave can make your project more frustrating than fulfilling. If you must insist on such a type of fabric for color reasons, etc., then use the paper piecing construction technique. This method stabilizes your fabric and will make possible the use of a looser weave than is normally desirable.

Stay away from heavy-weight fabrics such as wools and corduroys, etc. These fabrics tend to be stiff and hard to handle when piecing or doing applique. In addition, the resulting quilt will be very stiff and will not drape or fold properly over a miniature doll bed. If your small quilt is for a wall, then a heavier weight fabric might be suitable.

Do use medium weight, good quality, 100% cotton fabrics. These handle well and tend to have a minimum of fraying problems. By keeping all the fabrics you use in one quilt the same weight, you will find that your piecing and applique work will go more smoothly and look better.

Always wash all the fabric that you will be using in your project in hot water with a good quality soap. I like to wash my fabrics in a special soap, "Orvus®," which is recommended for safe use on old fabrics. But no matter what soap you are using, be sure to *thoroughly* rinse your fabric to remove all soap residue. This residue can remain in your fabrics and cut their life span. You will be spending many hours making an heirloom miniature, don't let time destroy your work.

Surface Design:

It would seem logical that I would suggest small prints, but large prints are not to be overlooked. A quilt composed of prints which are all the same size or scale can become very boring. Large prints can provide extra interest by drawing attention to certain areas or features of the quilt. They can also add drama to the overall effect of the completed quilt. Since these quilts are small, special effects can be achieved by using the fabric surface designs to draw attention to the quilt.

A special trick available to miniature quiltmakers is the use of one or two large prints to provide the look of many different fabrics. For example, if a large flower print is used as in Fig. 4, and a template measuring 1" square is placed on the fabric and moved around to different areas, many different options for pattern and color emerge.

Figure 4

An additional advantage of using fabric this way is that all the pieces cut from the same cloth will recombine effectively in the quilt. The reason for this is simple: the manufacturer of the cloth had already designed these shapes and colors to blend together. All the quiltmaker has to do is move them around and create new shapes and patterning.

All types of surface designs are suitable in miniature, i.e., flower patterns, squiggly lines, geometric shapes, and wide or narrow stripes. Each of these has its own special use. Pinstripes can be used in the pin-wheel pattern to make the blades appear to spin. Wide stripes can be cut apart to create sashings or borders. Geometric shapes can be used to represent objects that the manufacturer never intended. Fig. 5 shows a peacock which was cut from the border print next to it. Fig. 6 shows a basket which was created without any piecing, and Fig. 7 shows a vine-covered cottage made from a flowered pinstripe while the bushes around its foundation are from a fan-shaped print by Laura Asheley®.

In order to help you better visualize the possibilities of a piece of fabric, try cutting a 1" square

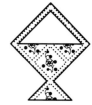

Figure 5

Figure 6

Figure 7

Figure 8

of clear plastic to take along with you on your buying trips to the quilt store. When you get there, place your square on the fabric you are considering and move it around the surface to see what shapes and objects you can discover. In this way, you will find that ½ yard of fabric can be equal to many different pieces of fabric without the additional cost!

Color:

Keep the color scheme for a miniature quilt simple. Too many different colors within the small size of these quilts makes it hard for the eye to focus and enjoy the design and workmanship of the quilt. Do not feel that only two or three colors per quilt is proper either. Often fabric of only two colors can look flat and uninteresting when used alone in a quilt.

The easiest way to determine a color scheme is to select a multi-color print fabric. This type of fabric provides the quilt with a third dimension effect, even without the quilting that will come later, and they can be the source of the colors which will compose the quilt. For example, using an overall print fabric that has green vines, flowers in two shades of salmon, blue-purple flowers, and yellow or gold centers on a light green background provides many colors to be drawn out and used throughout the entire quilt. Note the contrast of the dark, medium and light shades in the black and white illustration of this fabric, Fig. 8.

Include highlight and accent colors within your quilt. A miniature is not really different than a large quilt when it comes to color, the same rules apply.

I do not give "the" colors to use with each pattern in the "how to" section. The reason for this is that I believe each quiltmaker should use the color choices that most please her or him. A project is more likely to be finished if it pleases its maker. If, however, you feel that you need some direction for starting your miniature, use the color plate section included in Part I to help you in your decision making.

TEMPLATES

I like to use plastic for my templates. I prefer the "see through" types so that I can be sure to center the designs accurately on each pattern piece. Window templates of metal or cardboard also work well.

Since we are quilters, we tend to make our templates by cutting the shapes out with scissors. I find that there can be too much wobble or variation when using scissors. I prefer to use a craft knife and a metal ruler and over cut each side of the template. If you do not try to cut through the plastic all at once, but rather score the lines (by repeating several times), the template will drop out and be very accurate without any nicks or bumps.

Be sure to measure and mark all templates very accurately. The width of a pencil line can be critical when working in miniature. I recommend using a mechanical pencil of 5 mm width or finer for marking the template plastic. An error of ¹/₁₆" over only 16

pieces becomes a full one inch discrepancy, a large error on a quilt that only measures 16"!

CONSTRUCTION TECHNIQUES
Rotary Cutter-Strip Piecing Method

The invention of the rotary cutter and the various types of rulers and equipment that go with it have revolutionized patchwork. No longer are tedious hours needed to cut out pattern pieces. Instead, quick and accurate piecing can be achieved with excellent results.

I made the Nine Patch, Geese in Flight, Friendship, Log Cabin Variation, and One Patch Scrap quilts all using the rotary cutter system. The construction of these quilts is not limited to this technique, however, and all could be constructed using traditional means.

To use the rotary cutter system, first cut strips the desired width and length from your fabric as shown in Fig. 9. These strips are then sewn together in pairs or larger quantities as each quilt requires, Fig. 10. The arrows indicate the direction of the machine stitching; by sewing alternately up and down, you can reduce warpage of the finished blocks.

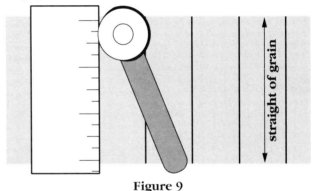

Figure 9

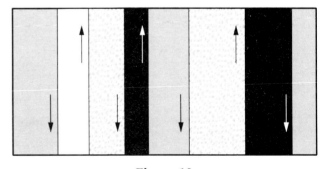

Figure 10

In Fig. 11, a square template is placed over the two-seamed strips and the rotary cutter used to cut out the square. If the square is placed so that the two opposite points are centered over the seam, a pieced square of two right triangles will result. This is a fast, easy and extremely accurate way to make pieced squares in miniature.

Fig. 12 shows three strips sewn together and cut apart at regular intervals. By sewing the same three fabrics together in reverse order of set A to form set B, cutting them apart at regular intervals and then sewing the strips together as in C, a nine-patch block can easily be constructed.

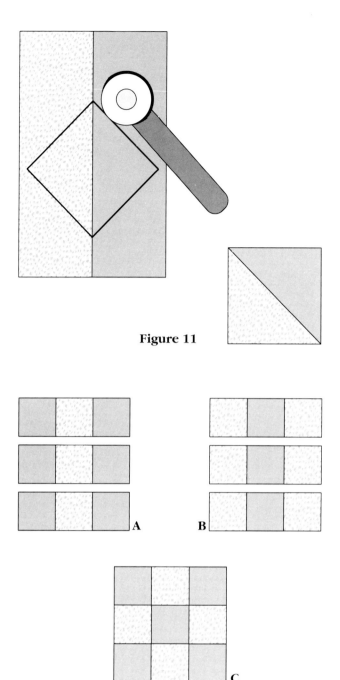

Figure 11

A **B**

C

Figure 12

Paper Piecing

This technique is best used when precision is paramount. It takes a little extra time but guarantees a high quality result in the completed quilt. Traditionally paper piecing has been used when constructing hexagons or other non-traditionally shaped pieces, but it can be used for any shape. It can be especially helpful when dealing with curved shapes such as the Rose Dream quilt.

First cut "papers" to the exact size of the completed patch. I find that paper is too thin for piecing the small pieces necessary in a miniature quilt. I prefer to use file or index cards. They are a little stiffer and hold their edge for better accuracy. I especially like the quality of the file cards that can be bought in discount chain stores. They are a bit thinner than the ones from a quality stationery store and are easier to stitch through.

After cutting the "papers," cut your fabric piece adding the standard ¼" seam allowance to all edges. I prefer to make a plastic template for the papers and a separate one for the fabric pieces.

Place the paper in the middle of the wrong side of the fabric patch and fold the fabric edges over the paper, see Fig. 13. The edges are then basted in place, using quilting thread for basting. I find that quilting thread is thicker and therefore easier to remove. After all the pieces are basted the assembly begins.

With right sides together, whipstitch seams together using

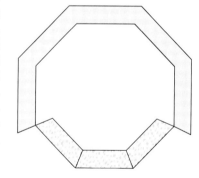

Figure 13

all purpose sewing thread, Fig. 14. Try not to stitch through the papers. About 10 stitches to ½" is adequate. After all seams are assembled, clip threads and remove basting stitches and all papers. Be careful not to clip into fabric when removing basting stitches. Also, take care to remove ALL papers. If you find one when quilting the top, it will be too late to remove it!

PIECING

Whether piecing by machine or hand in the traditional assembly fashion or by quick-piecing techniques, I always use a standard quilters' ¼" seam. I do not trim the seams after construction except where multiple seams come together, such as at a star's mid-point, where I grade the seams and cut off any excess. I like to leave the standard ¼" seams because I feel it gives additional strength to the quilts.

The one exception I made to this rule was for the ⁵⁄₁₆" hexagons. I felt that by trimming the seams to ⅛" widths after assembly, the bulk was reduced and the quilt became softer and easier to drape over a bed.

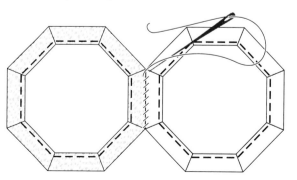

Figure 14

APPLIQUE

The first problem that occurs when appliqueing a small piece of fabric is fraying. This difficulty can be magnified by the use of poor quality fabric. Be sure to test the fabric you intend to use for your applique on a piece of waste background material; then you will know how it handles and if too much fraying develops when the edges are turned under. I cannot stress the use of a test piece too strongly. It is so much easier to try a sample and discover problems than to find you have committed yourself to an impossible project.

General instructions for applique usually state ¼" seam allowances. Because of the size of the pieces to be appliqued in miniature quilts, however, I recommend ³⁄₁₆" to ⅛". The smaller of the two widths is used for acute angles when a minimum tuck under is all that can be successfully managed, Fig. 15. I cut out all my applique pieces with the standard ¼" but trim down as I go along, adjusting to the reaction of the different fabrics and shapes. Be careful to keep your applique stitches close enough together to keep all edges securely tucked in.

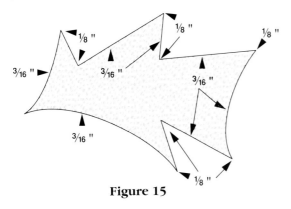

Figure 15

I favor the use of a blind hem stitch but an invisible stitch, embroidered buttonhole stitch, or even a very small whip stitch would also be suitable. Since these quilts are small, it is important to get a lot of three dimensional feeling in the quilt. I do this by means of multi-layers of applique, the addition of embroidery stitches, or by stuffing special features such as yo-yos. Care should always be taken to consider whether it is best to use applique or to substitute another technique, such as embroidery, cross stitch, quilting, etc.

If you are adept at making ⅛" wide bias binding, then go ahead and do so. But if not, then why not use two strands of embroidery floss in a chain stitch to create stems or vines.

To position applique correctly, I fold my background fabric in half and press with an iron, then fold again and press, then open and refold on the diagonals, pressing lightly, Fig. 16. This technique will give you a center point and "lines" for

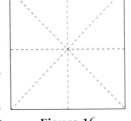

Figure 16

positioning your applique pieces. I prefer this method to marking with one of the dissolving chemical markers now on the market. Since these markers are still new and haven't had the test of time, their use on an heirloom project could jeopardize the quilt's longevity.

YO-YOS: STUFFED AND UNSTUFFED

I have used yo-yos on the Rose of Sharon quilt to create the center areas of my flowers and for small bud-like shapes. They add a rich third dimension to the applique and embroidery on a quilt. The idea is not new, however, it was used on old 19th century quilts, especially for grapes (stuffed) and for flowers (unstuffed).

A yo-yo is made by cutting out a circle, turning the edge over ⅛" and stitching through the turned over area with a basting stitch. Use all purpose sewing thread to match color of the yo-yo. The gathering thread is then drawn up tight and ended off, Fig. 17. After gathering, use the needle to pull the fabric out evenly into a symmetrical circle and press lightly with an iron.

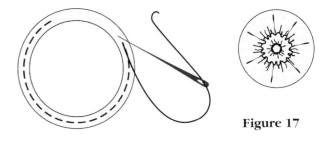

Figure 17

If a stuffed yo-yo is desired, before completing the gathering step insert a piece of batting or poly-fil™ the size of a pea into the yo-yo. Continue gathering and end off as for unstuffed yo-yo.

Still another trick with a yo-yo is to proceed as described above for the unstuffed yo-yo, but before finishing the gathering step, add a circle of contrasting color fabric to the inside of the yo-yo and end off as before. This center circle should be the size of the completed yo-yo. If the yo-yo is to represent a flower, a yellow, orange, or dark green color can be used for the center circle. This will serve to look like the stamen or pistil of the yo-yo flower, Fig. 18.

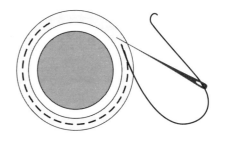

Figure 18

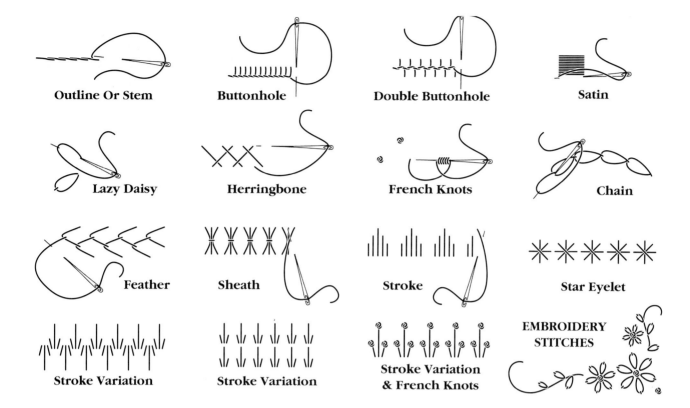

Outline Or Stem   **Buttonhole**   **Double Buttonhole**   **Satin**

Lazy Daisy   **Herringbone**   **French Knots**   **Chain**

Feather   **Sheath**   **Stroke**   **Star Eyelet**

Stroke Variation   **Stroke Variation**   **Stroke Variation & French Knots**   **EMBROIDERY STITCHES**

EMBROIDERY

To keep the embroidery work in scale with the size of the quilts, I use only two strands of cotton embroidery floss. Any brand of embroidery floss will do, although I like DMC® because it has a slight sheen which adds richness to the finished project, especially on a Crazy quilt.

When producing a crazy quilt, certain standard stitches were used but sometimes the quiltmakers modified or invented their own stitches to fill odd-shaped spaces. Feel free to experiment on your crazy.

SEWING PROBLEMS

Applique does not turn smoothly. Either too much seam allowance, or a poor choice of fabric for the applique, or unwashed fabric with too much sizing.

Frayed edges on applique. Too little seam allowance or too loose a weave of fabric. If the fabric choice is too loose a weave but "just right" for color or other needs, use paper piecing technique to stabilize the material.

Seams tear out on pieced work. Seam allowances are not a full ¼" or fabric choice has too loose a weave. Paper piecing technique can be used instead of traditional American seaming technique.

Applique doesn't turn and frays. Perhaps the piece you are trying to applique is too small. Embroidery or another needlework technique could be used instead of applique.

BAGGIE SYSTEM

Through teaching many miniature quilt classes and having hundreds of students, I have found a little trick I'd like to share.

Zip Loc® bags must have been invented with the miniature quilter in mind. If you put all your cut out fabric pieces in such a bag, your paper (if paper piecing) in another bag and completed blocks in yet a third, and then place all the mini Zip Locs® into one large Zip Loc,® you can carry your entire quilt project anywhere and everywhere without the fear of losing any of your precious pieces.

I call this my "baggie system." I find it works well and I always grab my bag before leaving the house. I even keep it with me in the car. Some of us live in areas where traffic jams can last for one to two hours without moving at all! What a satisfying feeling it is to complete three or four entire quilt blocks while waiting for the traffic problem to clear!

What about doctor's offices? I always bring my baggie with me and work while I await my turn. Don't forget the dentist's office, and luncheons and banquets, or dull and boring meetings! Just pull out your "baggie system" and get to work. Don't let time be your enemy; miniatures are just perfect for busy people like ourselves.

BATTING

I recommend a thin polyester batting such as "Mt. Mist Quilt Light"® by Stearns and Foster or "Pellon Fleece"® (be careful, there are several grades and you want the thinnest one). Both of these batts allow a miniature to drape gracefully and quilt easily.

With batting, like all the rest of quilting items, your preferences will prevail, and there is no reason not to try different types of batting: cotton, cotton/poly, wool, flannel, and even silk. I have made a very successful doll house size miniature using silk batting. It was like quilting through butter. Remember, our quilting ancestors used whatever was on hand, so experiment to accomplish the "look" or "feel" you want in your quilt.

If you should have trouble with your quilt draping successfully, a trick used by some people making miniature quilts may help: place no batting on the sides of the quilt, only on the top of the bed surface.

I use batting throughout my quilt top and have not had trouble with my quilts draping successfully. I plan seams to come along the top edge of the mattress and this encourages the sides to fall softly. Another trick is to quilt the sides of a miniature quilt either vertically or diagonally, thereby forcing the quilt to drape well over the sides of the bed.

BACKING

The backing of a miniature quilt deserves careful thought. It is all too easy to think that "just any" piece of fabric will do for the backing. In the quilts of the early 19th century, chintzes and wonderfully interesting column prints were used. In the late 19th century ginghams and small calicoes (apron prints) were used. The backing of the quilt should relate to the quilt top in time period and color, and if a multi-color print is used, the use of different colors of quilting threads can be easily camouflaged.

I like to use stripes for the backings on my early 19th century style miniatures because they are somewhat reminiscent of the old column prints. For the late 19th century pieces I often use the new reprints of the 1880's style fabrics. I like the old look they give to my quilt, and the richness they provide over using a plain fabric.

PREPARING THE QUILT FOR QUILTING

I always add 2" on all sides to the dimensions of the top for both the batting and backing. By being this generous, I have allowed for any slippage that might occur during the quilting, (although a properly basted top should not slip during the quilting process). Also, the extra goods allow the quiltmaker using a Q-Snap® quilting frame to quilt all the way out to the edges of the quilt.

Prepare your miniature as you would a large quilt. Iron and lay out the backing. Then lay the batting on top and lay the quilt top over both. Baste through all three layers with the same care you would give a full-size quilt. Don't skimp on the basting because the quilt is small. It is important to stabilize the unit for the best quilting results.

MARKING THE TOP FOR QUILTING

If the quilting lines are straight, especially when filling in the background as in the Four Eagle or Princess Feather quilts, I prefer to use masking tape for marking my quilting lines. I use tape in the same width

as the quilting rows, ½" or ¼", and quilt down both sides of the tape. Then I move it over to the next rows to be quilted. Be careful because as you reuse the tape, it begins to stretch and warp. Once it starts to distort, discard that piece and take a new one. Remember never to leave the tape on a quilt overnight, or in the hot sun (at poolside or in the car for example), as it may leave a sticky residue. For these reasons, some quilters prefer to use drafting tape because it is less sticky than ordinary masking tape.

If marking a cable or other fancy quilting design, all the choices for marking a full-size quilt are available to the miniaturist. I prefer to stay away from water soluble and disappearing marking pens because of their chemical content and possible future damage to the quilt. There are many pencil and chalk-type choices available. Just remember, test a small sample first to be sure the markings can be safely removed.

QUILTING FRAMES

I'm always asked, "Do you use a quilt frame, and if so, which one?" The answer is yes. I have used a wooden hoop and found that it stretched the miniature too much on the bias. I prefer the Q-Snap® plastic frames. They come in several sizes and the pieces are interchangeable, giving the quiltmaker a lot of freedom. Because the pieces make either a square or rectangular frame, the quilt is not as easily pulled off grain and will hang straight when finished. And, as mentioned in the basting section, this type of frame allows the quilter to work out to the very edge of the quilt, thereby enabling the same quilting tension to be kept throughout the quilt.

QUILTING

From the very first planning of a miniature quilt, or any quilted work, consideration should be given to the quilting. Since these quilts are small and some patterns contain hundreds of pieces, there are many seams which means extra hard work when quilting.

I find several ways to cope with this problem. First, if I want a lot of quilting, I plan my miniature quilt to have as large areas as possible for the quilting. Two examples of this approach are the Four Eagles and the Rose of Sharon quilts. In the Four Eagles, the quilting has been done every ½" in parallel diagonal rows which fill the background area and allows the eagles to come forward and become the focus of the quilt while the background remains where it belongs, in the background, Fig. 19.

In the Rose of Sharon quilt, a different quilting technique was used. It is called stipple quilting and fills the background areas with quilting stitches that are ¹⁄₁₆" to ⅛" apart, Fig. 20. The effect is one which flattens the entire background and causes the unquilted areas to raise up and appear as stuffed work with additional filling. The stippling can be done randomly or around each shape as if echoing that shape, until all the background is filled with quilting. The back of a stip-

Figure 19

Figure 20

around the center square, thereby forming concentric diamonds, Fig. 21. This technique minimizes the seams one has to quilt through, however it does not eliminate them.

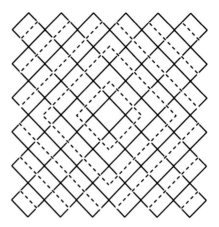

Figure 21

Since seams are a problem in these quilts, one is tempted to forego large amounts of quilting. I think this approach is in error. It is the quilting that makes a quilt a quilt. And it is the quilting that adds depth and dimension to any patchwork or applique design. Since the purpose is to capture the look and essence of the old quilts, it is important to remember that the originals were heavily quilted. To duplicate them, as much quilting as possible should be included in the miniature.

When quilting a miniature with small applique such as the Oak Leaves or when embroidered vines or stems are to be next to the quilting, be sure to consider the proportion between the quilting stitches and the work. Not everyone can quilt small enough (18 stitches or more to the inch) to keep the quilting stitches in scale with the applique or embroidery. Whenever I'm faced with this problem, I often only quilt close to the edge of the small work so that the quilting isn't immediately noticeable. The result is that I have provided the quilting the miniature needed without confusing the eye as to which it should focus on, the designs or the quilting.

I also find it confusing to the eye when contrasting color quilting thread is used. I always match my quilting thread to the background area or patch that I am quilting. This way the quilting becomes secondary to the design surface of the quilt as in full-size quilts, and allows the viewer to fully and more carefully enjoy the work.

pled quilt can become almost as interesting as the front because the shapes on the front become designs on the reverse, and the quilting stitches form all the patterning.

If, however, a patchwork such as the One Patch Scrap quilt is to be quilted, it can be approached in one of two different ways. The first choice would be to "quilt in the ditch" along the seam line of each piece. But care must be taken in the construction to press all seams to one side, not open, so that the lower edge has no extra layers of cloth. The quilting is done through this lower edge, along the seam line but not in it. Quilting in the seam can weaken it.

The second option, and the one I chose for my scrap quilt, is to quilt through the center of each row

TYING

Originally many quilts were not made as bedspreads or counterpanes, but as "blankets" for warmth, a strictly utilitarian purpose. As a result, many quilts received no quilting, but instead were tied. Wool yarn was used to make knots at even intervals across the quilt to hold the three layers together. There is no reason not to apply this technique to a miniature quilt.

I have used it on the hexagon quilts and the log cabin variation.

Sometimes I like the ties to show and do knotting on the front (Log Cabin Variation) with three strands of embroidery floss. Other times, as in the hexagons, I only use the tying to hold the layers together and use one or two strands of floss, knotting on the reverse side where it won't interfere with the graphic design of the top.

FINISHING TECHNIQUES

A. Backing brought over front:

Bring the backing fabric over the front edge of the quilt and tuck in the edges of the backing to form a ¼" wide binding, trimming backing fabric as necessary. For a professional look, miter all binding corners.

B. Tucking edges in:

Turn in front and back edges of quilt to the inside and slip stitch the edges together. Be sure to trim the batting ¼" narrower than the front and backing so that it will fit safely inside the edge without buckling.

C. Alternatives:

Use a *separate binding*, made either of straight of grain or bias strips.

Insert *piping* in between the front and back edges of the quilt. I have seen this technique used on quilts from the mid and late 19th century. Be sure to keep the piping in scale with the size of the quilt. There is a packaged small piping commercially available for use on baby clothes that would suit certain size miniature quilts. The *hand loomed tapes* used on the late 18th and early 19th century quilt edges can be imitated by the use of seam binding (preferably the older type which is quite thin and has a looser weave). Trim the quilt to even the edges, and apply the seam binding over both the top and back surfaces of the quilt, using a running stitch. End off by cutting the end of the binding ½" longer than needed, then fold raw edge to the inside and slipstitch the end of binding edge over the beginning edge.

The *scalloped edges* that were popular in the 1920's and 30's can also be achieved if care is taken in their planning.

Prairie points can be folded to fit a miniature quilt's edge.

Use *old lace or handmade tatting* to simulate the handmade fringes of the late 18th and early 19th century quilts. Many of these quilts were white on white counterpane types and would look excellent on a four-poster style doll bed.

Any edge or finishing treatment used on a large quilt can be used on a miniature, just remember to keep it in scale with your quilt.

SIGNING AND DATING

I'm a firm believer in signing and dating all quilts and quilted objects that a quilter makes. How easy our quilt heritage research projects would be if all the quiltmakers of the past had signed and dated their quilts! There is no reason not to sign your work. Be proud of what you have produced, and if your work is a gift for someone, they will be proud to have your name on it.

I always put my name, date, copyright symbol if appropriate, and number in the series on the back of each quilt, no matter what the size. Some of the quilts are embroidered with the information, Fig. 22, others are written in indelible ink on a separate label. I prefer, when possible, to mark directly on the quilt; a separate label can always get lost.

Figure 22

In order to further document my work, I keep a 5½" x 8" three-ring notebook with my original graphs, fabric swatches, and all pertinent information, (i.e., beginning and completion dates, number in the series, photos of each quilt, etc.). This log or "bible" will afford future historians a wealth of information, not only about the quilts but about their maker as well, and it will provide me with documented proof for my insurance company in case of an accident or theft claim.

It only takes a few minutes while you are making a quilt to write down the facts, but it can take ever so much longer if you wait until after the quilt is complete to try and remember all the information you will need to write down in your log. So stop right now, and buy a three-ring notebook for recording your work! Future quilt historians will thank you.

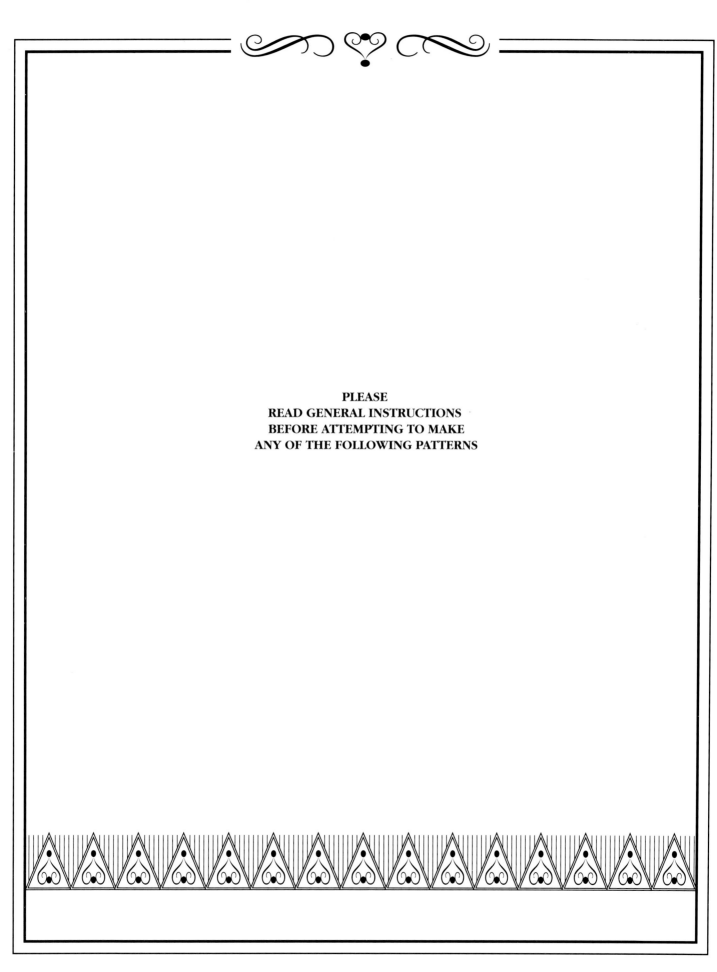

PLEASE
READ GENERAL INSTRUCTIONS
BEFORE ATTEMPTING TO MAKE
ANY OF THE FOLLOWING PATTERNS

Figure 23

NINE PATCH
Color Plate I

Dimensions: 15½" x 18½"
Number of Pieces: 320
Construction Techniques: pieced, rotary cutter
  and sewing machine
Fabrics: strong contrast between fabrics A & B
  and C & D. Medium contrast for solid
  blocks and half triangle border.

YARDAGE:
A & inner border- ¼ yd.
B- ⅜ yd.
C- ¼ yd
D- solid blocks & outer border- ¼ yd.
E- border triangles & backing- ⅝ yd

CUT:
7 strips- 1" wide of A
7 strips- 1" wide of C
9 strips- 1¼" wide of B
7 strips- 1" wide of B
3 strips- 1¼ wide of A
3 strips- 1¼" wide of C
20 squares- 2¼" (Z)- of D
18 triangles (W)- of E
4 triangles (V)- of E
2 strips- 1" x 15" of A, inner border
2 strips- 1" x 18" of A, inner border
2 strips- 1¼" x 20" of D, outer border
2 strips- 1¼" x 18" of D, outer border
rectangle- 18" x 21" of E, backing

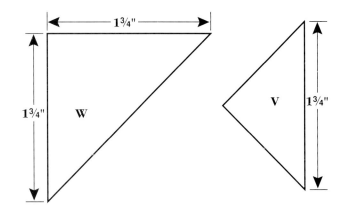

Templates do not include seam allowance.

DIRECTIONS:

Stitch strips together as in Fig. 24 and 25. Cut strips ABA and CBC into 1" widths. Cut strips BAB and BCB into 1¼" widths. Stitch these units together to form 15 blocks each of X and Y, Fig. 26.

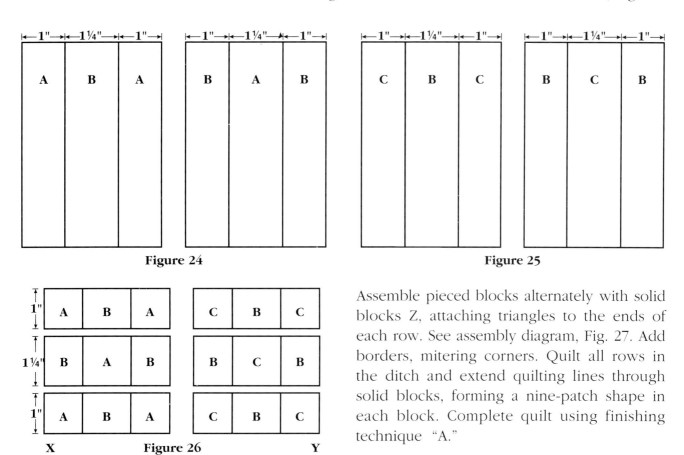

Figure 24

Figure 25

Figure 26

X

Y

Assemble pieced blocks alternately with solid blocks Z, attaching triangles to the ends of each row. See assembly diagram, Fig. 27. Add borders, mitering corners. Quilt all rows in the ditch and extend quilting lines through solid blocks, forming a nine-patch shape in each block. Complete quilt using finishing technique "A."

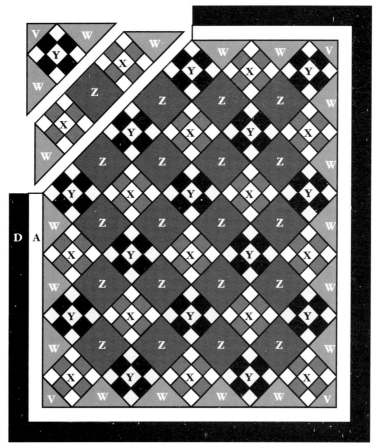

Figure 27

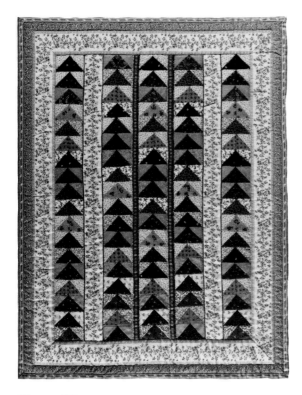

Figure 28

YARDAGE:
Assorted scraps
Sashings and border- ¾ yd.
Backing- ¾ yd.

CUT:
72- A
72- B
72- B in reverse
4 strips 18½" x width of stripe plus seam
   allowance for sashings
2 strips 24½" x width of stripe plus seam
   allowance for side borders
2 stripes 10" plus width of sashings, plus
   seam allowance for top and bottom
   borders
rectangle- 21" x 26", backing

SKILL LEVEL: *Beginner*

GEESE IN FLIGHT
Color Plate II

Dimensions: 19" x 24"
Number of Pieces: 278
Construction Technique: pieced, hand or
   machine
Fabrics: scraps, stripe for sashing and border

DIRECTIONS:
   Stitch patch A to both B's to produce block unit, Fig. 29. Stitch four rows of 18 geese each. Add sashings to geese rows. Add borders, mitering corners. Quilt all rows in the ditch along sashings and border edges. Complete quilt using finishing technique "A."

OPTIONAL: Quilting may be done around individual geese.

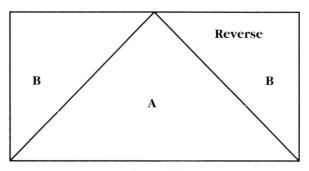

Figure 29

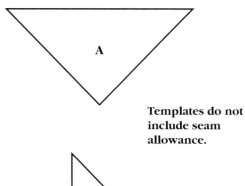

Templates do not include seam allowance.

30

Figure 30

YARDAGE:

A- 1 yd., background, border and backing
B- ⅜ yd., eagles and inner wheel
C- ½ yd., outer wheel and sawtooth border
D- ¼ yd., stars
E- ¼ yd., or scraps, eagle's claws

Cotton embroidery floss:

1 skein each: brown- branches
green- leaves
black- eye and beak

CUT:

(Only if using the quick-piece method of construction for Sawtooth)
11 strips- 1¼" x 18" of A
11 strips- 1¼" x 18" of C
otherwise you will need
76 triangles of A
76 triangles of C
plus
1- 18½" square of A, background
1- 22" square of A, backing and binding
4 eagles
1 inner wheel
8 feet (4 of each pattern)
8 large stars
1 center star
1 outer wheel

SKILL LEVEL: *Advanced*

FOUR EAGLES
Color Plate III

Dimensions: 20" x 20"
Number of Pieces: 176
Construction Techniques: applique, pieced, hand or machine, embroidery
Fabrics: Traditional colors are red or brown for eagles, yellow for stars, red and green for wheels.

Template does not include seam allowance.   **Sawtooth Border Template**

DIRECTIONS:

Using Fig. 30 as your guide, lay out applique motifs on background fabric and baste in place. Applique all designs down, starting with center star and wheels and continuing to each eagle and its stars.

If hand or machine piecing in the traditional method, piece sawtooth squares using template provided. If using the quick piecing method, seam A and C strips together. Cut into 76, 1½" squares. Sew these squares together in strips of 19 sawteeth each. Attach as shown in Fig. 30.

Embroider as follows:
olive branches- 2 strands, stem stitch
leaves- 2 strands, lazy daisy stitch
eagles' eyes- 2 strands, French knot
beak- 2 strands, stem stitch

Quilting: Follow directions given on pattern pieces. To achieve overall background quilting, quilt in diagonal rows ½" apart being sure not to quilt through the applique areas.

Complete quilt using finishing technique "A."

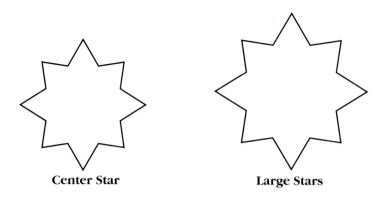

Center Star

Large Stars

OUTER AND INNER WHEELS
WITH QUILTING LINES (DASHES)

Templates do not include seam allowance.

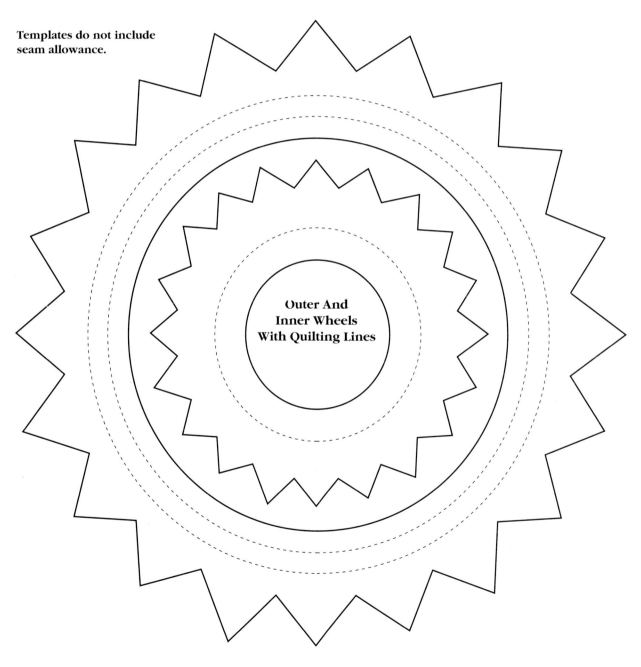

Outer And
Inner Wheels
With Quilting Lines

Eagle pattern piece with quilting lines
(dashes) and laurel leaf, eye and beak
embroidery.

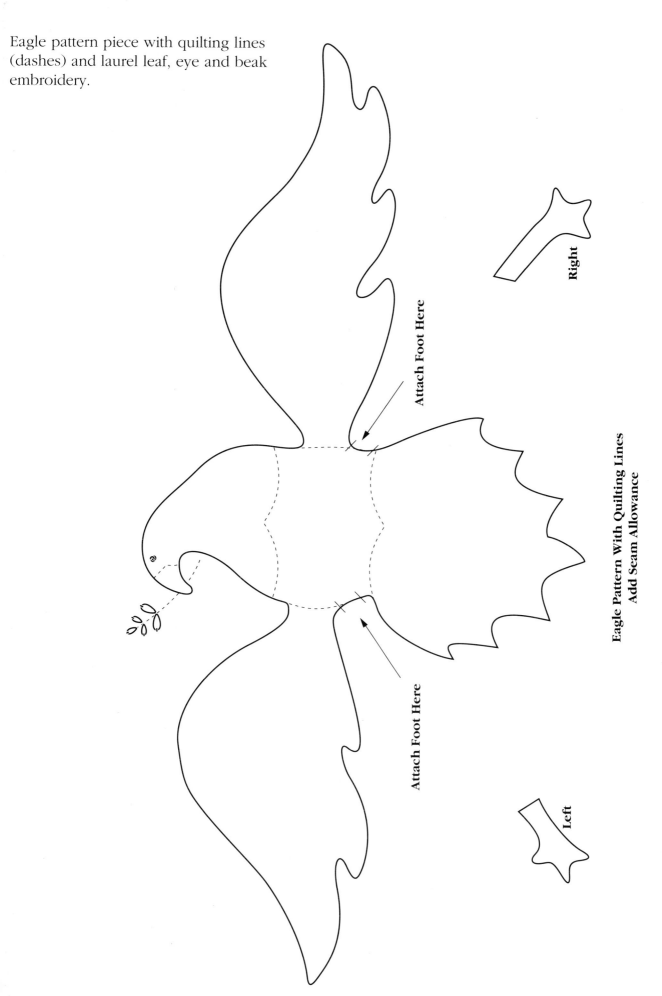

Attach Foot Here

Attach Foot Here

Right

Left

Eagle Pattern With Quilting Lines
Add Seam Allowance

Figure 31

YARDAGE:

Scraps or fat quarters of many different prints.
Background color in each block- ⅝ yd.
Muslin centers- ¼ yd.
Sashing and top triangles- ½ yd.
Side and bottom triangles- ⅜ yd.
Backing- 1 yd.

CUT:

196- A	5- D
196- B	13- E
49- C	4- F

Sashings: 1 strip 1¼" x 33½" (piecing when
necessary)
1 strip 1¼" x 29¾"
1 strip 1¼" x 26"
1 strip 1¼" x 22¼"
1 strip 1¼" x 18½"
1 strip 1¼" x 14 ¾"
1 strip 1¼" x 11"
1 strip 1¼" x 7¼"
40 strips 1¼" x 3½"

SKILL LEVEL: *Intermediate*

FRIENDSHIP
Color Plate IV

Dimensions: 25½" x 31"
Number of Pieces: 511
Construction Technique: pieced, hand or
machine
Fabrics: scraps or fat quarter, sashing and top
triangles should contrast well with blocks,
outside triangles should be slightly darker
than sashings; backing- striking or
complex pattern to add interest, richness,
and age; also used as binding.

DIRECTIONS:

Assemble block units as in Fig. 32. Sign
and date blocks, if desired, using a fine point
indelible pen, such as a permanent Pilot™
marker. Sew short sashing strips between
blocks. Sew long sashings to bottom of each
assembled row. Use assembly diagram, Fig.
33, for sashing and row construction.

When assembled, the top D templates will
extend beyond sides of quilt. Trim them to
square off corners.

Quilting: Quilt in the ditch around all
pattern pieces and sashing seams. Quilt inside
border triangles ⅝" from seams in a chevron
pattern; repeat shape ⅝" from previous row,
Fig. 34.

Complete quilt using finishing technique
"A."

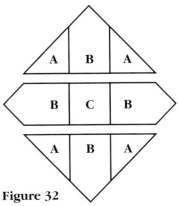

Figure 32

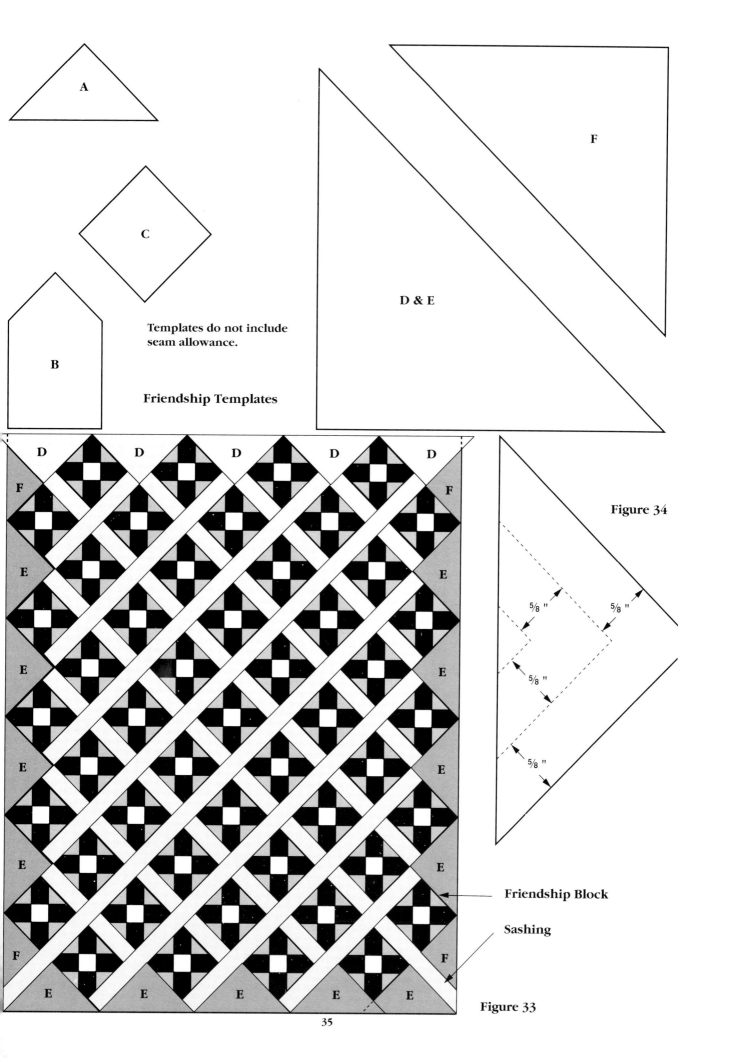

A

C

B

Templates do not include
seam allowance.

Friendship Templates

D & E

F

Figure 34

D   D   D   D   D

F   F

E   E

E   E

E   E

E   E

E   E

E   E

F   F

E   E   E   E   E

5/8 "   5/8 "

5/8 "

5/8 "

Friendship Block

Sashing

Figure 33

Figure 35

YARDAGE:

U- 1 yd., borders, flowers, hearts, backing and binding

V- ½ yd., vines, leaves and stems

W- ⅛ yd. or fat quarter, hearts for vine centers

X- ⅛ yd or fat quarter, buds in outer border

Y- ⅛ yd. or fat quarter, buds in center

Z- ⅝ yd., background

CUT:

16 of A from fabric U

4 of A from fabric Y

16 of B from fabric V

16 of C from fabric V

32 of D from fabric V

4 of E from fabric U

16 of F from fabric V

16 of G from fabric Y

16 of H from fabric W

8 of H from fabric U

24 of J from fabric V

8 of K from fabric U

8 of L from fabric X

8 of M from fabric U

4 strips 2¼" x 22" of U (outer border)

4 strips 1¼" x 12½" of U (inner border)

4– 5" squares of Z

4 strips 3½" x 18½" of Z

22" square of backing fabric

110" x ¾" of V, cut on the bias (vines-I)

SKILL LEVEL: *Intermediate to Advanced*

ROSE OF SHARON
Color Plate V

Dimensions: 20" x 20"

Number of Pieces: 201

Construction Technique: applique

Fabrics: reds or burgundy

pinks

greens

neutral for background

Directions:

Using Fig. 36 as your guide, applique pattern pieces B,C,D,F, and G onto each of the four center squares. To make stuffed center flower (pattern piece E), start to applique around the flower, when three-quarters of the way around, insert batting cut off from same pattern piece but without seam allowance added. (Poly-Fil® may also be used, but DO NOT stuff tightly.) Finish stitching around flower.

Figure 36

For pattern piece A, draw up circles into yo-yos (see General Directions). Stuff flower center A yo-yos with Poly-Fil® for a raised effect in the center of each flower.

When applique is complete, stitch the four center blocks together using ¼" seams. Add the four inner border strips (fabric U) and attach to center blocks, mitering corners.

Follow the same procedure for the four background strips which will be appliqued. Complete the construction of the top by adding outside border (fabric U) to all sides and mitering corners.

Using Fig. 37 as your guide, applique the bias strips, M, in place. Then add the remaining bias strips to create vine. Applique J,K,L, and H in place. Top is completed.

Quilting: Stitch around all applique pieces and along border edges. Mark the hearts in the four corners and stipple quilt in all background areas using the random or echo technique, see Fig. 38. The corner hearts will "puff-up" and will look like stuffed work.

Complete quilt using finishing technique "A."

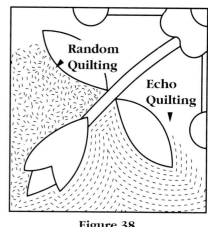

Figure 38

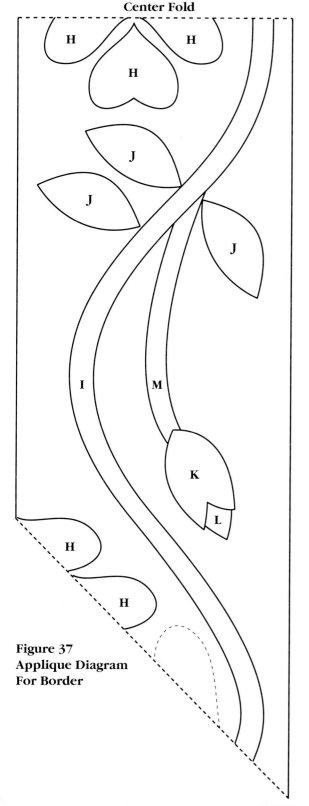

Center Fold

**Figure 37
Applique Diagram
For Border**

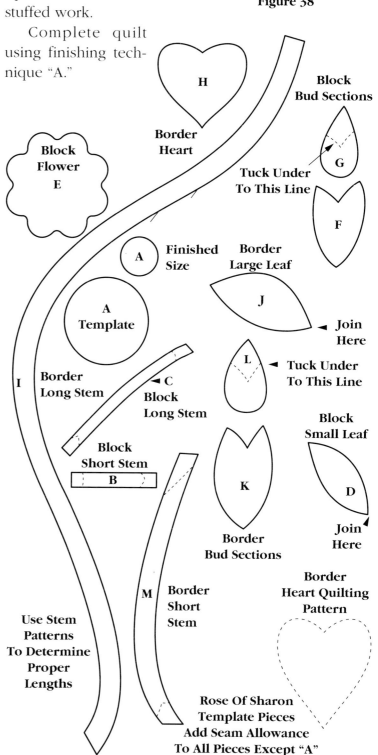

Figure 39

YARDAGE:

greens– A- ¼ yd. B- ¼ yd.
       C- ¼ yd. D- ¼ yd.
backing and squares- ⅝ yd.
sashings- ½ yd.

CUT:

16- 4" squares
 1- 19" square for backing
 2- strips 17" x 1"
 5- strips 16" x 1"
12- strips 4" x 1"
 6 leaves of A
 4 leaves of B
 4 leaves of C
 2 leaves of D

DIRECTIONS: Applique each leaf onto one of the 4" squares. Using Fig. 40 as an assembly guide, sew a short sashing strip to the bottom of the first three squares in each vertical row. Attach the 16" long sashings to the sides of all rows. Add the two 17" long strips to top and bottom of quilt to complete borders.

Quilting: Quilt around each leaf pattern and along the sashings and borders in the ditch. Complete quilt using finishing technique "A."

SKILL LEVEL: *Intermediate*

OAK LEAVES
Color Plate VI

Dimensions: 17" x 17"
Number of Pieces: 48
Construction Techniques: applique and
    pieced
Fabrics: four different greens
    white for backing and squares
    red or other color for sashings

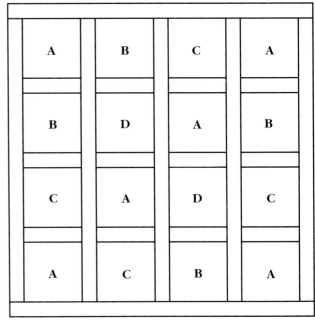

Figure 40 Quilt top assembly guide

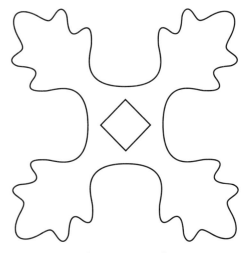

Oak Leaf Template

Seam allowance not included.

Figure 41

SUMMER GARDEN
Color Plate VII

Dimensions: 19¾" x 20¾"
Number of Pieces: 512
Construction Technique: paper piecing
Fabrics: 5 different prints for a soft old look,
    OR 5 solids for a contemporary look

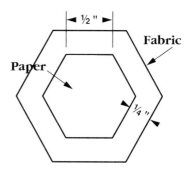

Summer Garden Templates

YARDAGE:

⅝ yd. of fabric A (includes backing)
¼ yd. of B
¼ yd. of C
¼ yd. of D
½ yd. of E

CUT:

142 hexagons of fabric A
 20 hexagons of fabric B
184 hexagons of fabric C
126 hexagons of fabric D
 40 hexagons of fabric E
22" x 23" rectangle of fabric A for backing
512 papers

DIRECTIONS: Fold fabric over papers and baste as described in the GENERAL DIRECTIONS. Assemble into rosettes from center as in Fig. 42. If you do not want a jagged hexagon shaped edge, applique the edges of all sides of the quilt to a narrow band of fabric A. After the top is assembled, remove the papers.

Because of all of the seams, no batting is necessary. It will drape more softly without it.

Tie with a single strand of embroidery floss in square knots on the reverse side.

Complete quilt using finishing technique "A."

A● B○ C◐ D◆ E○
Figure 42

Figure 43

YARDAGE:

⅛ yd. of A

⅛ yd. of B

⅛ yd. of C

⅛ yd. of D

⅛ yd. of E

⅛ yd. of F

¼ yd. for backing

CUT: 190 papers

34 hexagons of A

16 hexagons of B

48 hexagons of C

18 hexagons of D

42 hexagons of E

32 hexagons of F

9" x 9" square of backing

DIRECTIONS:

Follow assembly directions as for SUMMER GARDEN quilt, page 68. Use Fig. 44 as an assembly guide. Quilt will not be square. It is designed with cutouts for a four-poster bed. No batting is necessary. The quilt will drape more smoothly without it. Tie the quilt with double strands of embroidery floss in square knots on the reverse side. Complete quilt using finishing technique "B."

SKILL LEVEL: *Intermediate*

SHIMMERING STAR
Color Plate VIII

Dimensions: 7½" x 8" (doll house size)

Number of Pieces: 190

Construction Technique: Paper piecing

Fabrics: 6 different prints for top and 1 print for backing. A single plaid fabric can be used for all 6 prints if different areas of the plaid are used.

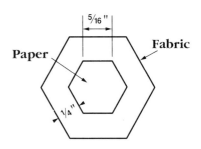

Figure 44

Figure 45

YARDAGE:

Scraps or ¼ yd. of 9 different fabrics

¾ yd. of backing fabric

¼ yd. of lightweight muslin

CUT:

3 strips 3½" x 18½" muslin

20" x 26" rectangle of backing fabric

2 strips 1½" x 18½" for sashings

4 strips 3½" x 18" for borders

Cut various fabrics from templates, trying not to make two alike so as to give more interest to the quilt.

CRAZY
Color Plate IX

Dimensions: 18" x 23½"

Number of Pieces: 54

Construction Technique: applique

Fabrics: light and medium weight velvet, sateen, moire, taffetta, ribbons, silks. Purchased embroideries may be used either with or instead of doing fancy embroidery designs.

DIRECTIONS:

To each of the three muslin strips, stitch the patches in the sequence provided in Fig. 46. Place the resulting strips so that the two outside rows are in the same top to bottom order and reverse the top and bottom order for the middle row.

Attach the completed strips to the sashing strips, using Fig. 45 as a guide. Add side borders, then top and bottom borders. It is not necessary to miter the corners.

Embroidery: Using two strands of embroidery floss and the embroidery stitches shown in the GENERAL DIRECTIONS, embroider over all seam lines. Laces and trims can be hand or machine stitched to the seam lines if you do not wish to embroider. Using the special embroidery designs provided, fill in the crazy patches with your choice of designs and colors. Don't hesitate to be creative and invent or vary standard stitches. Add embroidery designs that come in packages from fabric stores, or old or new laces, etc. Experiment, that is what CRAZY quilts are all about!

Quilting: Traditionally, crazy quilts are not quilted because there isn't any batting placed inside them. You can take a few tacking stitches to keep the back and front from separating, if desired.

Complete the quilt using finishing technique "A."

Daisies

Peacock Feather

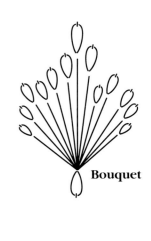

Bouquet

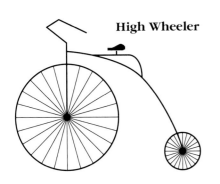

High Wheeler

Staff With Notes

Fan Shape

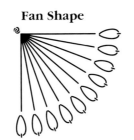

Spider Webb

Fern

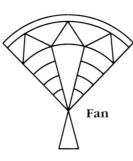

Fan

Stars

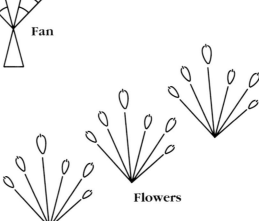

Cattails

Flowers

Butterfly

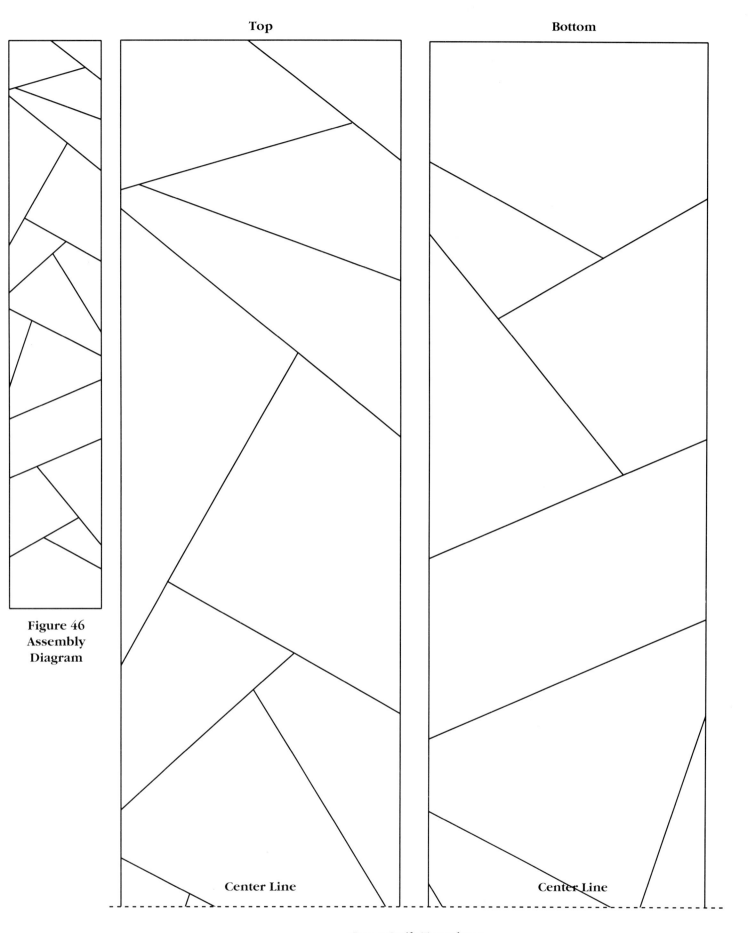

Top

Bottom

**Figure 46
Assembly
Diagram**

Center Line

Center Line

Crazy Quilt Templates
Templates do not include seam allowances.

Figure 47

SKILL LEVEL: *Beginner*

YO-YO
Color Plate X

Dimensions: 9½" x 11½"
Number of Pieces: 238
Construction Technique: yo-yos (see
    GENERAL DIRECTIONS)
Fabrics: dark- A
        medium- B
        medium light- C
        light- D

YARDAGE:

A- ¼ yd.

B- ¼ yd.

C- ¼ yd.

D-¼ yd.

CUT:

Cut circles 1¾" in diameter as follows:

40 of A

106 of B

52 of C

40 of D

DIRECTIONS:

Using assembly diagram Fig. 48 for color placement, make the quilt by assembling yo-yos in pairs on the reverse. Use matching color thread and a whip stitch. After each row is constructed, press lightly with iron. Assemble rows. No batting or quilting is needed. Quilt is complete. A lining may be added to the reverse, if desired.

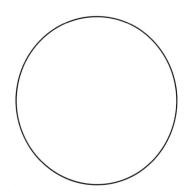

Yo-Yo Template
Template includes seam allowance.

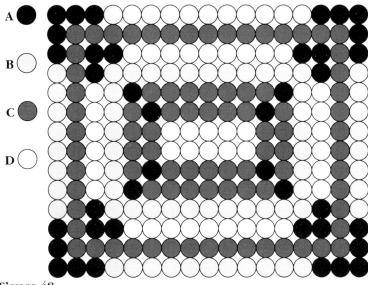

Figure 48

Figure 49

LOG CABIN VARIATION
Color Plate XI

Dimensions: 15" x 18"
Number of Pieces: 62
Construction Technique: pieced
Fabrics: If prints are used, the resulting quilt
     will have a 19th century look.

     reds- medium and dark
     blues- light and dark
     green- dark
     brown- medium
     yellow
     novelty type print (horse shoes,
          umbrellas, etc.)
     geometric print- light background

YARDAGE:

¼ yd. of A (dark red)

¼ yd of B (light blue)

¼ yd. of C (dark blue)

¼ yd. of D (light geometric)

¼ yd. of E (medium brown)

¼ yd. of F (yellow)

¼ yd. of G (novelty print)

¼ yd. of H (green)

⅝ yd. of J & backing (medium red)

CUT:

1 of template 1 of fabric A
2 of template 2 of fabric B
2 of template 3 of fabric H
2 of template 4 of fabric D
2 of template 5 of fabric A
2 of template 6 of fabric E
2 of template 7 of fabric C
2 of template 8 of fabric F
2 of template 9 of fabric D
2 of template 10 of fabric E
2 of template 11 of fabric B
2 of template 12 of fabric H
2 of template 13 of fabric E
2 of template 14 of fabric J
2 of template 15 of fabric F
2 of template 16 of fabric C
2 of template 17 of fabric J
2 of template 18 of fabric G
2 of template 19 of fabric H
2 of template 20 of fabric B
2 of template 21 of fabric C
2 of template 22 of fabric H
2 of template 23 of fabric G
2 of template 24 of fabric E
2 of template 25 of fabric D

(continued)

2 of template 26 of fabric I
2 of template 27 of fabric B
2 of template 28 of fabric F
2 of template 29 of fabric J
2 of template 30 of fabric C
1 of template 31 of fabric E
1 of template 32 of fabric A
1 of template 33 of fabric H

DIRECTIONS:

Seam pattern pieces 2 to top and bottom of center rectangle. Add side pieces 3, 4, 5, etc. in numerical sequence. Logs 31, 32, and 33 are stitched to top of quilt only. Use diagram Fig. 50 as your assembly guide.

Batting and quilting may be added to this quilt, especially if being made as a wall decoration. The original does not contain batting nor is it quilted. It is tied in square knots on the front with three strands of embroidery floss, creating an old tied-comforter look.

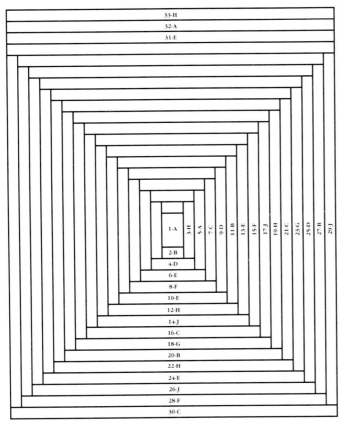

Figure 50

Templates
do not include
seam allowance.

**Log Cabin
Templates**

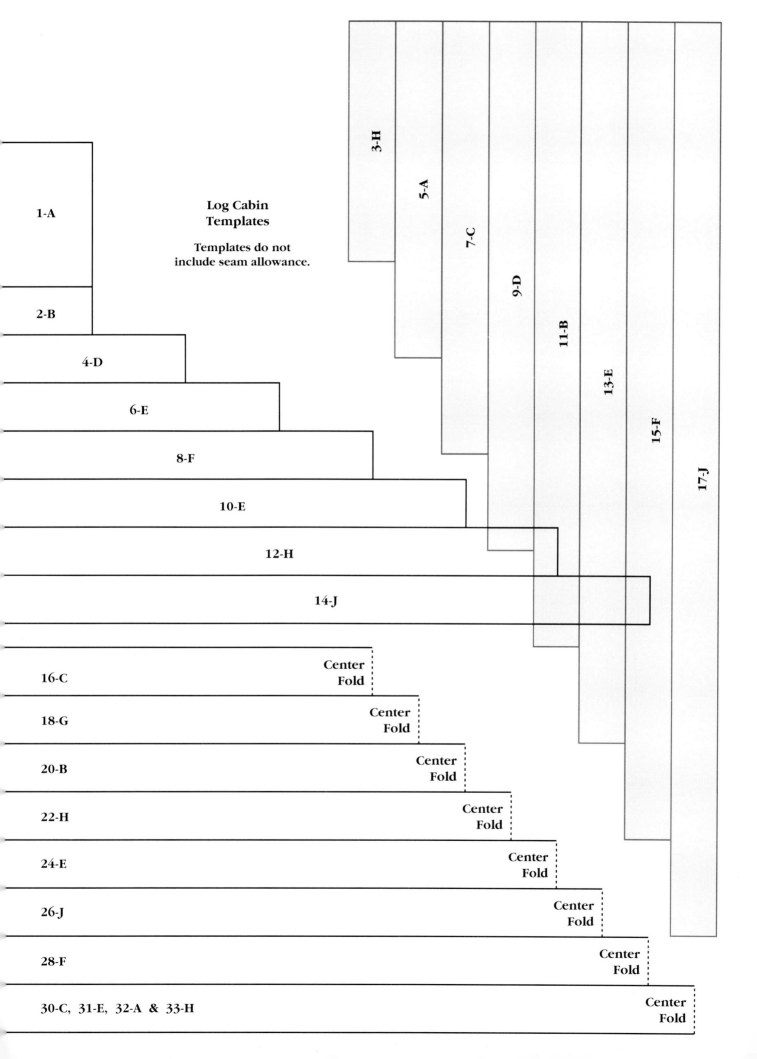

Log Cabin
Templates

Templates do not
include seam allowance.

1-A

2-B

3-H

5-A

7-C

4-D

6-E

9-D

8-F

11-B

10-E

13-E

12-H

15-F

14-J

17-J

16-C   Center
              Fold

18-G   Center
                  Fold

20-B   Center
                      Fold

22-H   Center
                          Fold

24-E   Center
                              Fold

26-J   Center
                                  Fold

28-F   Center
                                      Fold

30-C, 31-E, 32-A & 33-H   Center
                                          Fold

Figure 51

YARDAGE:
scraps
⅝ yd. for backing

CUT:
421 1½" squares
22" square for backing

One Patch Scrap Template
Add seam allowance to template.

ONE PATCH SCRAP
Color Plate XII

Dimensions: 20" x 20"
Number of Pieces: 421
Construction Technique: pieced
Fabrics: all colors and in varying intensities
    (light, medium, dark)

DIRECTIONS:
    Assemble the squares in rows, staggering the placement of colors and the light and dark intensities. Row 1 is comprised of 29 squares. Each subsequent row pairs will diminish by 2 squares, i.e., rows 2A and 2B contain 27 squares, rows 3A and 3B contain 25 squares, etc. Refer to Fig. 52 for assembly guide. The edges will be zigzag-shaped and can be cut straight using ruler and rotary cutter or scissors.
    Quilting: Quilt in the ditch around center square and through the middle of the next squares forming a diamond shape. Continue in this fashion until the entire surface has been completed.
    Complete quilt using finishing technique "A."

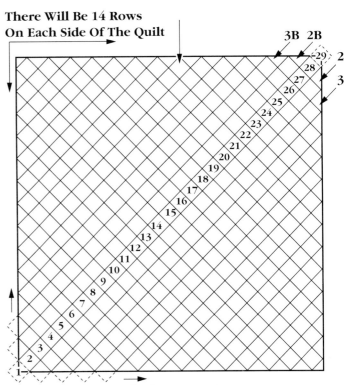

There Will Be 14 Rows
On Each Side Of The Quilt

Trim Excess From Blocks
To Make A Smooth Edge   **Figure 52**

Figure 53

YARDAGE:

½ yd. of A
1 yd. of B, includes backing

CUT:

42 of template 1 of fabric A
42 of template 1 of fabric B
21 of template 2 of fabric A
21 of template 2 of fabric B
42 of template 3 of fabric A
42 of template 3 of fabric B

Innermost border:
2 strips 1" x 20" of fabric B
2 strips 1" x 23" of fabric B

Middle border:
2 strips 1" x 21" of fabric A
2 strips 1" x 24" of fabric A

Outer border:
2 strips 1" x 23" of fabric B
2 strips 1" x 26" of fabric B

24" x 27" rectangle of B for backing

Papers:
84 of template 1
42 of template 2
84 of template 3

SKILL LEVEL: *Intermediate*

ROSE DREAM
Color Plate XIII

Dimensions: 22" x 25"
Number of Pieces: 222
Construction Technique: paper piecing
Fabrics: two colors, strong contrast

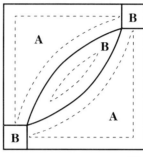 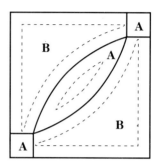

Figure 54

DIRECTIONS: Cover papers with fabric and prepare as in GENERAL DIRECTIONS. Whip stitch pieces together to make block units as in Fig. 54. Whip stitch block units together in rows, alternating units until there are 6 across and 7 rows down. Add borders, mitering corners.

Quilting: Quilt around pattern pieces 1 and 2, ¼" inside seam lines. Quilt diagonally through corner squares, 3. See Fig. 55.

Figure 55

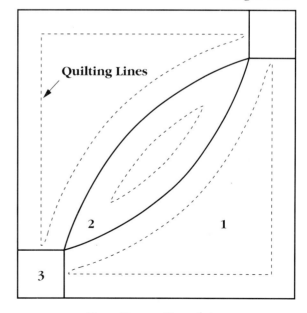

Rose Dream Templates
Actual Size Of The Paper Templates
Add Seam Allowance To Fabric Templates

Figure 56

YARDAGE:

¾ yd.- A (includes backing)

⅛ yd.- B

scraps- C

⅜ yd.- D-borders

CUT:

28- A

28- B

140- C

2 strips 3½" x 28½" from fabric D

2 strips 3½" x 22½" from fabric D

20" x 24" rectangle from fabric A

DIRECTIONS:

Assemble the fan blocks by piecing in units as in diagram, Fig. 57. Sew the blocks together in diagonal rows; see assembly diagram, Fig. 58. Add borders and miter corners.

Quilting: Quilt all seams in the ditch. In the arc over the fan, quilt ¼" inside seam lines, echoing the arc shape, Fig. 57. Using the cable quilting pattern provided, quilt the borders. Complete the quilt using finishing technique "A."

SKILL LEVEL: *Intermediate*

GRANDMOTHER'S FANS
Color Plate XIV

Dimensions: 18" x 22"

Number of Pieces: 200

Construction Technique: pieced

Fabrics: scraps or a planned color scheme

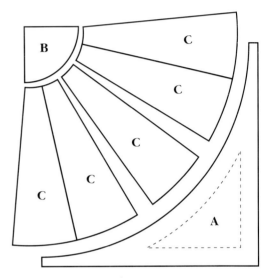

Figure 57

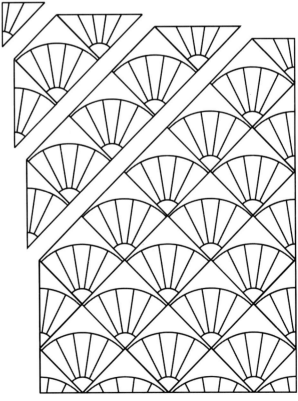

Figure 58

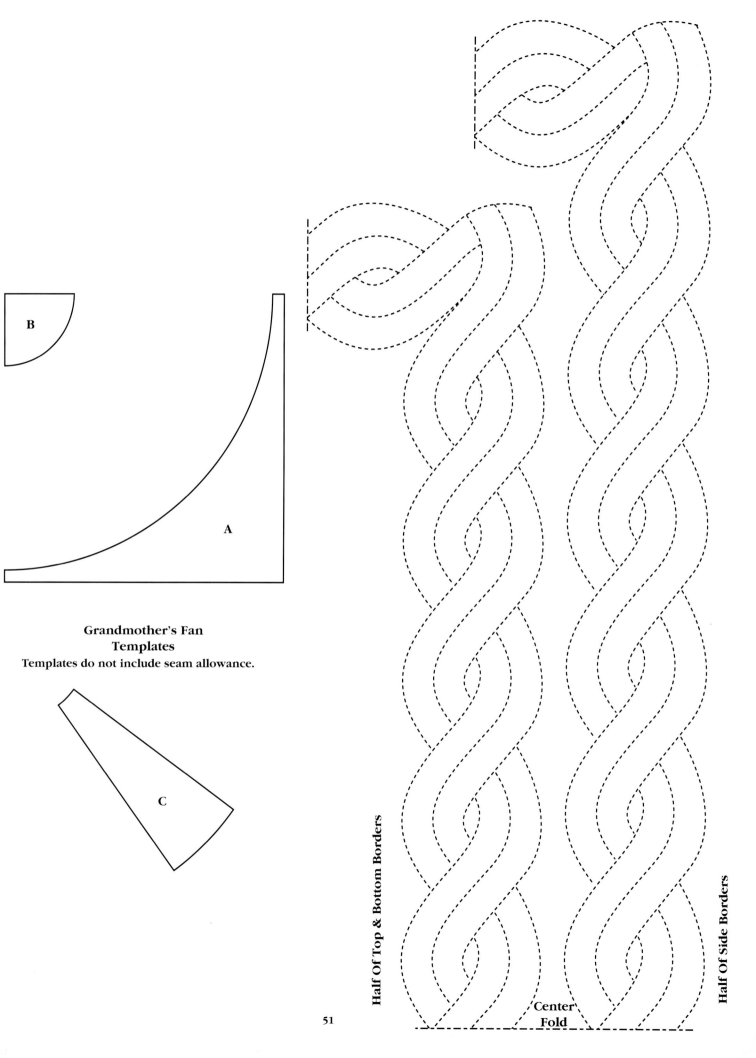

B

A

**Grandmother's Fan
Templates**
Templates do not include seam allowance.

C

Half Of Top & Bottom Borders

Half Of Side Borders

Center
Fold

51

Figure 59

CHINESE COINS
Color Plate XV

Dimensions: 17" x 23"
Number of Pieces: 58 (approximate)
Construction Technique: pieced
Fabrics: 19 different solids

DIRECTIONS:

Sew the many patchwork pieces together forming four rows, each 18½" long. Attach these rows to the sashing strips. Next attach side and top borders. Add the wide border strip to bottom.

Quilting: Quilt two rows ¼" apart through center of sashing strip. In pieced rows, quilt two parallel rows the length of the strip ½" from seam lines, Fig. 60.

For borders, use clamshell quilting patterns provided. See Fig. 61.

Complete quilt using finishing technique "A."

YARDAGE:

scraps or remnants
¼ yd. for sashings
¼ yd. for borders
¾ yd. for backing

CUT:

1 strip 2½" x 17½" for top border
2 strips 2½" x 18½" for side borders
1 strip 3½" x 17½" for bottom border
5 strips 1½" x 18½" for sashings
19" x 25" rectangle for backing
strips of 17 different solids, 2½" wide and
    varying widths at different angles

Figure 60

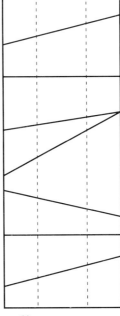

Figure 61

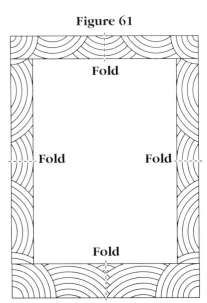

Left Side

Right Side

Bottom

Sides

Top

Center Fold
Mirror To Complete

Center Fold
Mirror To Complete

Center Fold
Mirror To Complete

Figure 62

PRINCESS FEATHER
Color Plate XVI

Dimensions: 20" x 20"
Number of Pieces: 314
Construction Techniques: applique and
    pieced
Fabrics: 2 contrasting colors, prints or solids,
    and light or neutral for background

YARDAGE:

¾ yd. fabric A (includes backing)

⅜ yd. fabric B

⅜ yd. fabric C

CUT:

1 template 1 of fabric A
8 template 2 of fabric B
4 template 3 of fabric A
4 template 3 of fabric B
76 template 4 of fabric A
148 template 4 of fabric B
72 template 4 of fabric C
4 template 5 of fabric A
16½" square for background
22" square for backing

DIRECTIONS:

Alternating colors, applique feathers to the background. Piece star and applique over feather stems. Applique circle over star center. Cut away excess fabric from back of applique work. Piece border blocks and attach to sides, Fig. 63.

Quilting: Quilt around all appliques and along seam lines in stars and border pieces. Quilt background in diagonal rows ¼" apart throughout background and into light triangles in outside border. Quilt ¼" inside seam lines in triangular-shaped areas in the outside row of border, Fig. 63.

Complete quilt using finishing technique "A."

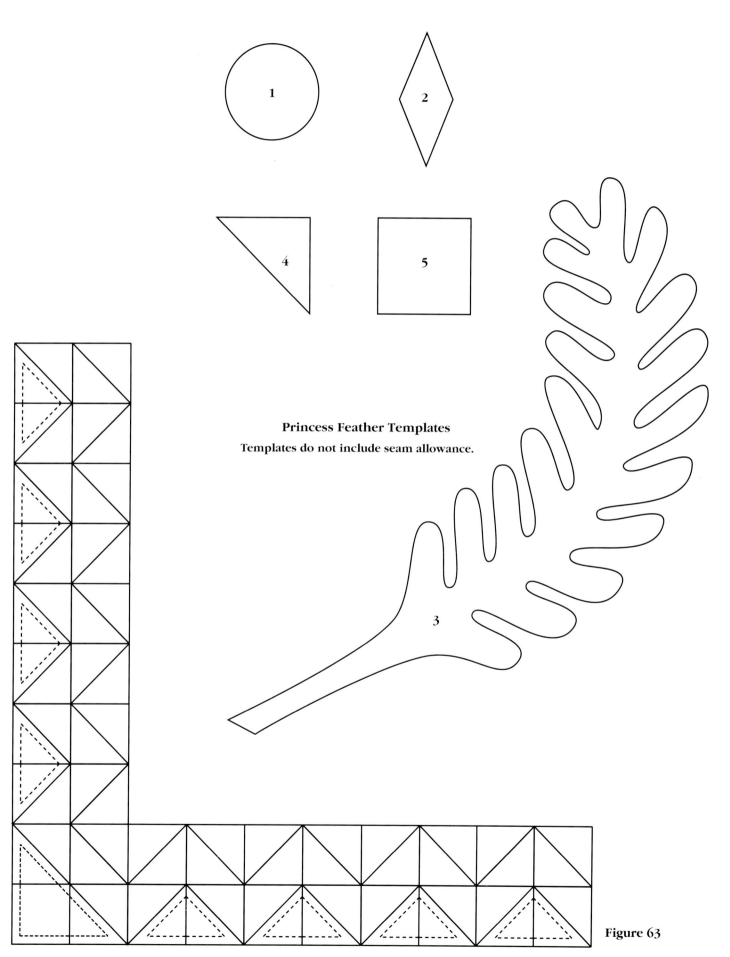

Princess Feather Templates
Templates do not include seam allowance.

1

2

4

5

3

Figure 63

Figure 64

HAWAIIAN "KAMAKANI KAILI ALOHA" Color Plate XVII

Dimensions: 20" x 20"
Number of Pieces: 3
Construction Technique: applique
Fabrics: strong contrasting solid colors

YARDAGE:

⅝ yd. of fabric A- applique and backing

⅝ yd. of fabric B- background

CUT:

1- 20" square of A
1- 20" square of B
1- 22" square of A (backing)

DIRECTIONS:

Using the 20" square of A, fold and press into quarters and then eighths (see GENERAL DIRECTIONS). Place pattern piece 1 on folded fabric with diagonals and straight edges of fabric along dotted lines on patterns. The point, X, should be at the point of the folded fabric. Trace around the template and add ³⁄₁₆" seam allowance. Repeat above procedure for pattern piece 2, Fig. 65. Carefully cut out shapes with SHARP scissors. Do not unfold until time to baste onto background square. Unfold carefully, DO NOT PRESS.

Using the 20" square of fabric B (background), fold and press as before. Place center motif on background carefully aligning the diagonals, being careful not to stretch the piece out of shape. Repeat for border motif. Using thread to match motif, stitch in place starting with the inside cut out areas. Keep your stitches small and even. At tight turnings, clip and adjust width of seam allowances and closeness of your stitches as necessary. After the applique is complete carefully press the top.

Quilting: Echo quilting is a traditional Hawaiian technique. Quilt around the applique designs close to edges. Then quilt ¼" inside and outside the applique, following the applique's shape. Continue in like manner until the entire surface is covered.

Complete quilt using finishing technique "A."

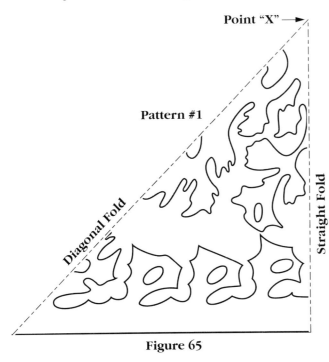

Point "X" →

Pattern #1

Diagonal Fold

Straight Fold

Figure 65

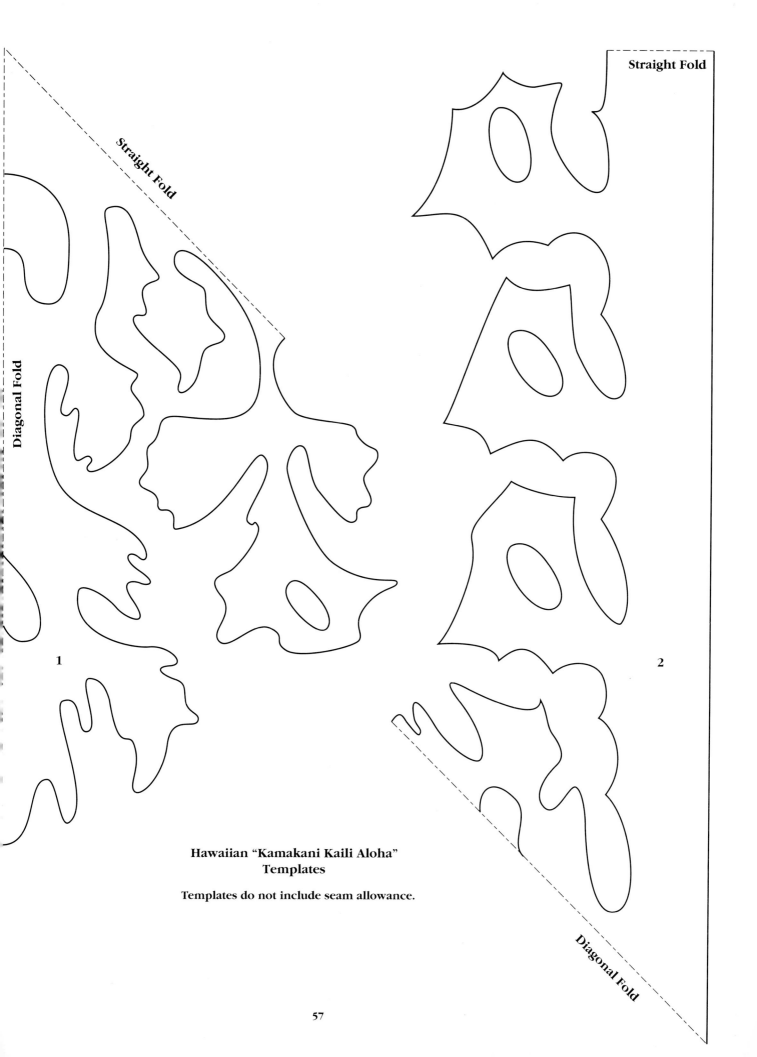

Straight Fold

Straight Fold

Diagonal Fold

Diagonal Fold

1

2

Hawaiian "Kamakani Kaili Aloha"
Templates

Templates do not include seam allowance.

FOOTNOTES

1 Bishop, Robert. "New Discoveries in American Quilts." E. P. Dutton Co. Inc., NY 1975. p. 118 plate 81.

2 Lipsett, Linda Otto. "Remember Me: Women and Their Friendship Quilts." Quilt Digest Press, San Francisco, CA 1985. p. 63.

3 Martin, Judy, "Pieces of the Past." That Patchwork Place, Inc., Bothell, WA 1986. p. 14.

4 Association of Community Arts Councils of Kansas, "Kansas Quilts – An Exhibition of Antique and Contemporary Quilts from Kansas Collections." p. 33 plate 40.

BIBLIOGRAPHY

Association of Community Arts Councils of Kansas. "Kansas Quilts – An Exhibition of Antique and Contemporary Quilts from Kansas Collections."

Bacon, Lenice Ingram. "American Patchwork Quilts." William Morrow & Co. Inc., 1973.

Bishop, Robert, "New Discoveries in American Quilts". E.P. Dutton Co. Inc., NY, 1975.

Bishop, Robert and Elizabeth Safanda. "A Gallery of American Quilts." E.P. Dutton Co. Inc., NY, 1976.

Bishop, Robert, William Secord, Judith Reiter Weismann. "Quilts, Coverlets, Rugs and Samplers." Alfred A. Knopf, NY, 1982.

Colby, Averil. "Patchwork." Charles T. Branford Co., Newton Centre, MA, 1958.

Colby, Averil. "Patchwork Quilts." Charles Scribner's Sons, NY, 1965.

Ferrero, Pat, Elaine Hedges and Julie Silber. "Hearts and Hands." The Quilt Digest Press, San Francisco, CA. 1987.

Finley, Ruth E. "Old Patchwork Quilts and the Women Who Made Them." Charles T. Bradford Co., Newton Centre, MA, 1957.

Haders, Phyllis. "The Warner Collector's Guide to American Quilts." Main Street Press Division of Warner Books Inc., NY, 1981.

Holstein, Johathan. "The Pieced Quilt." New York Graphics Society, Boston, MA 1973.

Houck, Carter and Myron Miller, "American Quilts and How to Make Them." Charles Scribner's Sons., NY, 1975.

Hughes, Trudie. "Template Free Quiltmaking." That Patchwork Place, Bothell, WA, 1986.

Johnson, Bruce, "A Child's Comfort." Harcourt, Brace, Jovanovich in association with the Museum of Folk Art, NY, 1977.

Katzenberg, Dena S. "Baltimore Album Quilts." Baltimore Museum of Art, 1981.

Kiracofe and Kile. "The Quilt Digest." Kiracofe and Kile, San Francisco, CA, 1983.

Lasansky, Jeanette. "In the Heart of Pennsylvania." The Oral Traditions Project of Union County Historical Society, Lewisburg, PA, 1985.

Leone, Diana. "Fine Hand Quilting." Leone Publications, Los Altos, CA, 1986.

Lipsett, Linda Otto. "Remember Me, Women and Their Friendship Quilts." Quilt Digest Press, San Francisco, CA, 1985.

McMorris, Penny. "Crazy Quilts." E.P. Dutton Co. Inc., NY, 1984.

Martin, Nancy. "Pieces of the Past." That Patchwork Place, Inc., Bothell, WA, 1986.

Nelson, Cyril I and Carter Houck. "The Treasury of American Quilts." E.P. Dutton Co. Inc., NY, 1982.

Nicholas, Marion. "Encyclopedia of Embroidery Stitches, Including Crewel." Dover Publications Inc., NY, 1974.

Safford, Carleton L. and Robert Bishop. "American's Quilts and Coverlets." E.P. Dutton Co. Inc., NY 1980.

ABOUT THE AUTHOR

Tina Millen Gravatt currently resides in Philadelphia, Pennsylvania. She has been successfully quilting since 1973 when she made her first baby quilt. Since then she has produced so many quilts, wallhangings, pillows, etc. that she has lost count of the number. She sews on an old Kenmore sewing machine in her second floor studio which she shares with her calico cat, Cleopatra.

Since embarking on the miniatures in 1985, she has completed 59 of them. Her doll bed collection, used for the display of her quilts, numbers 56. She often jokes of needing an extra "bed" room for them.

A self-supporting single mother of two daughters, she teaches and lectures both nationally and internationally.

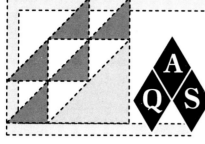

A Special Invitation To Join The
American Quilter's Society

Membership Benefits Include:

American Quilter magazine, published four times a year,
exclusively for members of the society

Free admission to the annual AQS quilt show in Paducah, Kentucky
Our show has become one of the largest in the country
and one of the few offering cash prizes.

AQS Update, a bi-monthly newsletter to keep members
informed of upcoming shows, workshops, special events,
awards and recognition of achievements across the country

Membership discounts on your favorite quilting books and more

Free Listing In *Quilts For Sale*, a full color catalog
of quilts published four times a year, and promoted nationally

Membership Card & Pin

Share the joy of quilting...
from one quilter to another.

To begin receiving **American Quilter** magazine...and all the
benefits of American Quilter's Society membership...just call

1-800-626-5420

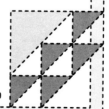

#2501 - 1 Year Membership $15.00
#2502 - 2 Year Membership $27.00
#2503 - 3 Year Membership $40.00

American Quilter's Society • P. O. Box 3290 • Dept B • Paducah, KY 42002-3290